"The Latin phrase *nota bene* (n.b.) means 'note well!' Sr. Melannie Svoboda not only knows that phrase—she lives it. In *Abundant Treasures* we have fifty-one n.b.'s that will enrich our spiritual treasure troves."

† Bishop Robert Morneau
Auxiliary Bishop of Green Bay

"In *Abundant Treasures* Sr. Melannie Svoboda offers accessible meditations to today's Everyman and Everywoman. These meditations come from life's daily gifts and they range from kindness to whimsy. Anyone who wants a spiritual companion for the new millennium could do no better than to turn these pages."

William J. Bausch
Author, *The Yellow Brick Road:*
A Storyteller's Approach to the Spiritual Journey

"Sister Melannie herself is one of God's treasures as she so ably demonstrates here. She delights us, encourages us, and surprises us with her inspiring insights and homey images. A wonderful book!"

Gwen Costello
Author, *A Prayer Primer for Catechists and Teachers*

"We are once again indebted to Sr. Melannie Svoboda for opening our eyes to the beauty of life. Prophetlike, she guides us in fiftey-one brief essays, from Abundance to Zeal, to consider the Spirit's gifts and qualities with fresh insight, with a new slant. She peppers the chapters with stories, poignant quotations, and references to Jesus' words and example.

"We discover, for example, that we should define 'compassion' by what we do, not by how we feel. She explains 'fear of the Lord' as dazzlement, the awe we experience in God's presence. She will have you think twice about the role of pleasure in life and about the surprising meaning of 'piety'. Prayerful reflection on these gifts, as Sr. Melannie presents them, is the spiritual tune-up we seek to keep our faith and love vibrant."

John van Bemmel
Author, *Prayers About Everyday Stuff*
Co-Author, *100 Prayers for Making Faith Connections*

MELANNIE SVOBODA

Abundant Treasures

Meditations on the Many Gifts of the Spirit

TWENTY-THIRD PUBLICATIONS
BAYARD ⊕ Mystic, CT 06355

Twenty-Third Publications/ Bayard
185 Willow Street
P.O. Box 180
Mystic, CT 06355
(860) 536-2611
(800) 321-0411

ISBN:0-89622-999-8
Library of Congress Catalog Card Number: 99-75666
Printed in the U.S.A.

Dedication

To Kathleen (Kay) Koehler:
from the day we met on the playground
at St. Felicitas School over 40 years ago,
you have been a gift of the Spirit in my life,
one of my abundant treasures.

Contents

Abundant Treasures

Introduction

Tucked away on a bookshelf in my room is a small black notebook given to me several years ago by my mother. In it my mother has written down dozens of items around her house that she wants to pass on to her children and grandchildren after her death. The items are listed in alphabetical order, each with a brief description. One of the first items, for example, is this:

Gold bracelet. My mother's. Initials SK stand for Stella Krbec. Given to her about 1910. Note engraving.

The little book goes on to list a whole array of other items: a glass pitcher that once belonged to my great-aunt, some doilies crocheted by my grandmother, my grandfather's shaving mug, my father's high school ring. In a way, the book lists my family heirlooms, those cherished keepsakes that form part of my inheritance. Those keepsakes, though not necessarily worth a lot of money, are very precious to me, for they unite me with the very life and spirit of my ancestors.

As Christians, we are members of another family, the community of believers. This family not only stretches around the globe, it also extends back into history. We Christians, therefore, are recipients of a magnificent heritage of all those believers who have gone before us. But what exactly have we received from our ancestors of the faith? What constitutes our spiritual heritage? A listing of our "spiritual heirlooms" would be quite extensive, no doubt, and would include things such as sacred Scripture, the Eucharist, the other sacraments, traditional prayers, spiritual writings, devotion to the saints, and so forth. The list would also include the gifts of the Holy Spirit.

When I say "gifts of the Holy Spirit," many of us immediately think of the traditional seven gifts found in the Septuagint version of Isaiah 11:1–3 which are wisdom, understanding, counsel, fortitude, knowledge, piety, and fear of the Lord. Although the Latin Fathers usually referred to the gifts of the Spirit as seven, the Greek Fathers showed little concern for limiting their number to seven. Rather, they followed in the footsteps of St. Paul who listed many other gifts of the Spirit besides the traditional seven. Throughout his letters, Paul writes of gifts such as healing, inspired speech, teaching, service, prayer, and prophecy.

This is a book on the gifts of the Holy Spirit. But I use the word "gifts" in a broad sense. I include the traditional seven gifts, yes, but I also write about other gifts such as attentiveness, beauty, diversity, intimacy, leadership, and patience. The book even includes some gifts of the Spirit not always thought of as gifts: bereavement, common sense, desire, guilt, failure, relaxation, and levity. Sometimes I also give other names to the traditional gifts. Knowledge, for example, becomes intimacy; fear of the Lord is dazzlement. (You will have to read the chapters to learn why I changed their names!)

The fifty-one gifts are arranged in alphabetical order for easy reference. Each chapter begins with an appropriate quotation from a wide variety of sources. Next comes the meditation on that particular gift, a meditation rooted in both Scripture and daily life. At the end of each meditation there are a few questions to facilitate your personal reflection on that gift in your own life. And finally, each chapter concludes with a short prayer to encourage your prayerful dialogue with God about each gift. The book can be used privately or for group sharing.

There is also a topical index at the end of the book to help you navigate through the book. If you are looking for the gift of "love," for example, you will not find a chapter with that title. But if you consult the index, you will see there are many chapters that deal with that topic. If you are looking for something on justice, you will be directed to piety.

I call this book *Abundant Treasures,* for the gifts of the Holy Spirit are certainly treasures given to us by a God whose goodness knows no bounds. The abundance of God is celebrated in Psalm 16, a prayer of gratitude for God's blessings. How privileged are we to be the recipients of so great a heritage, a heritage that includes these gracious gifts of the Holy Spirit. And how privileged are we to pray the words of this anonymous and exuberant ancestor of our faith:

O Lord, it is you who are my portion and my cup;
It is you yourself who are my prize.
The lot marked out for me is my delight:
Welcome indeed the heritage that falls to me! (Psalm 16:5–6)

May this book help us all to welcome with ever greater enthusiasm the precious gifts of the Holy Spirit into our everyday lives!

Abundance

We have all benefitted from the rich blessings he brought to us—blessing upon blessing heaped upon us.
—John 1:16

Astronomers tell us there are between 50 billion and 100 billion stars in our galaxy. (A billion is 1,000 millions!) What's more, there are an estimated 50 billion galaxies in the universe. (The known universe, that is.) That means, if every galaxy has 50 billion stars (a conservative estimate), then there are 50 billion times 50 billion stars swirling around in space, that is, 2,500,000,000,000,000,000,000 stars! That is a heck of a lot of stars!

From the sheer number of stars alone, it is pretty obvious: Our God is a God of abundance. It seems, when it came to creating stars, at least, God got carried away. God couldn't stop with two or three or even a few dozen stars—as reasonableness would dictate. No, God had to keep churning them out, star after star after star. And it is not just with stars that God got carried away. The numbers are just as mind boggling when it comes to other things God made—like grains of sand, snowflakes, dandelions, bees!

God's apparent lack of restraint when it comes to creating things is but a symptom of a deeper "problem": God lacks restraint when it comes to loving, too. In fact, God is *most* unrestrained when it comes to loving. Put another way, God cannot love except abundantly.

We see this abundance of God's love demonstrated throughout the Old Testament. The Chosen People turn away from God again and again. What does God do? Does God throw up his divine hands in disgust and cry, "Enough already!" and zap those Israelites into kingdom come? No, God continues to love them, taking them back again and again and again. There seems to be no end to God's love. There is no end to God's love.

Isn't that what Jesus was all about? Jesus' life was one big Show-and-Tell of God's abundant love. What is the parable of the prodigal son, for example, but a proclamation of the abundance of God's love? What is Jesus' agony in the garden but a graphic demonstration that, when all is

4

lost and nothing makes any sense any more, the only proper thing to do is to fall backwards into the arms of the God of Abundant Love—and trust, trust, trust.

We are made in the image and likeness of God. We are disciples of that Show-and-Tell Jesus. As such, we are called to love abundantly, too. What is more, the Holy Spirit is eager to give us this gift of abundant love. But we must say yes to it. And sometimes we do. (Thank God!) We love abundantly by reaching out to the unattractive, by being faithful to a commitment year after year, and by forgiving someone who has wronged us. But sometimes we say no to the gift of abundant love. This happens when we put limits on our love: "I will love this well-behaved little child, but not that smelly, old homeless man!" Or when we hold back our love: "I can't love you right now. Come back next year." Other times we squirrel away our talents and resources, we block our ears to the cry of the poor all around us, or we dole out our love with an eye-dropper.

No, we are meant to love abundantly—just as God loves—with sweeping gestures, to the max, as if there were no tomorrow. What enables us do this, of course, is our personal experience of God's abundant love in our own lives. And our belief that this God of abundance, this Spirit of Jesus, now truly loves through us!

In her book, *The Writing Life*, Annie Dillard says this: "One of the few things I know about writing is this: spend it all, shoot it, play it, lose it, all, right away, every time. Do not hoard what seems good for a later place in the book, or for another book; give it, give it all, give it now....Anything you do not give freely and abundantly becomes lost to you. You open your safe and find ashes."

That is good advice for writing. That is also good advice for loving.

How have I experienced the abundance of God's love in my life? What hinders me from loving more abundantly? What helps me?

✚ Spirit of Jesus, fill me with your abundant love!

Anger

If we had been better people, we would have been angrier oftener.
—Richard Bentley

Anger has bad press these days—especially in some religious circles. For many, anger is a negative emotion, a shameful thing. After all, anger makes individuals speak hurtful words, scream profanities, throw dishes, brandish baseball bats, and even kill.

That may be true. Sometimes. But sometimes anger can be good. It can even be a gift of the Spirit. Just look at Jesus. He got angry not once, but a number of times. In his anger, for example, he called the Pharisees some pretty terrible names: You hypocrites! (Matthew 23:13); You blind fools! (Matthew 23:17); You brood of vipers! (Matthew 12:34); You white-washed tombs! (Matthew 23:27). He even got angry at Peter one day and called him Satan (Mark 8:33). But perhaps the clearest display of Jesus' anger occurred the day he cleansed the Temple.

Even the phrase "cleanse the Temple" is a euphemism—as if Jesus strolled in with a little plastic pail and began to mop the corridors or something. Not so. When Jesus cleansed the temple, he stormed up the steps like a madman, brandishing a whip around his head. He screamed at the moneychangers while hurling over their tables and chairs. Then he stood guard at the entrance, breathing heavily, eyes glaring, his whip poised, ready to block anyone who dared to carry anything through those portals. That's what the cleansing looked like.

Some people are quick to say, "But it was okay for Jesus to get angry. After all, he was God." Others excuse his anger by saying, "His anger was justified." The truth is, many of us are uncomfortable with or even embarrassed by this image of a raging, quasi-maniacal Jesus. We prefer a gentler Jesus, the Good-Shepherd-cuddling-a-white-wooly-lamb-Jesus. But we must be honest: the raging Jesus is just as real as the cuddling Jesus. And sooner or later we must come to accept this anger in Jesus— as well as the anger in ourselves. We must see how, at times, anger is the only fitting response to a situation. Anger can be a friend.

Anger is our friend when it shakes us out of our complacency. There is an innate tendency in many of us to let things be, to not rock the boat, to keep things just as they are—no matter how ridiculous, awful, or unjust. That is where anger can come in. If we spot something that is not right, our spontaneous anger might just be the spark we need to act, that is, to do something about making things right—or at least better. (Anger, of course, never justifies violence. Jesus was pretty clear on that. "Turn the other cheek," he said. Remember? And his own acceptance of the terrible violence done to him on Calvary speaks louder than any words he could have uttered.)

Anger is our friend too when it draws our attention to something that may be wrong within ourselves. Sometimes our anger is a red flag alerting us to a deeper problem we may be avoiding. Persistent anger can be a way of cloaking other emotions that might be too painful for us to name, let alone deal with—such as hurt, grief, loneliness, or fear. When we are angry, then, it makes sense not to dismiss it immediately. Rather, we might want to sit with our anger for a while, walk around it, and explore its roots. We might be surprised at what we discover. Sometimes a good friend or counselor can help us explore our anger.

A few years back I found myself complaining to my spiritual director about a particular situation in my life. Month after month, I complained—with considerable anger. Then one day I said to her, "You know, I'm sick and tired of hearing myself complain about this thing." (No doubt she was, too!) Then I found myself saying something else: "I guess I'd better either do something about this thing, or shut up already!" My anger eventually led me to take some definite steps, albeit difficult steps, to better the situation I was in.

There is a point where patience ceases to be a virtue. And a point where anger becomes one.

What makes me angry? Have I ever sat with my anger, walked around it, or explored its roots? If so, what did I find?

✟ Jesus, you got angry too. Help me to befriend my anger so it may lead me to work more actively for the coming of your kingdom.

Attentiveness

To pay attention, this is our endless and proper work.
—Mary Oliver

There's an old joke about a farmer who bought a mule that was supposed to listen to whatever it was told to do. The farmer told the mule to pull his plow, but the mule refused to budge. The farmer yelled at the beast, pleaded with him, cajoled him, but to no avail. Frustrated, the man called the previous owner to come over. "I thought you said this mule listened to whatever you told him to do," he complained. "But he won't listen to me." Without saying a word, the former owner walked away and returned with a big stick. He took the stick and swatted the mule once across the rear end. Immediately the mule began to pull the farmer's plow. "See?" said the man, "He listens real good. But first you've got to get his attention."

The word "attention" is an interesting word. Did you ever notice that, in English at least, we say *pay* attention? Ordinarily we don't say *do* attention or even *give* attention. Certainly we never say *loan* attention. No, attention is something we *pay*. The verb "pay" implies that every time we focus our consciousness on someone or something, we pay a price.

And we do: our time and energy. Now, both our time and energy are very valuable. They are also limited. Consequently, we cannot pay attention to everything that clamors for our attention on a given day or we would go insane. No, we have to be selective in what we are attentive to. So we find ourselves saying things like this: "Tonight I'll spend time with my son...Tomorrow I'll clean the bathroom...This Saturday I'm going to a movie...Today I have no time to watch TV."

Advertisers know all about selective attention. They also know (like the farmer in the story) that the first step to getting us to do what they want us to do (buy their cheese or deodorant, for example) is to get our attention. So they are ingenious at finding ways to get it. Take TV ads, for instance. Advertisers use catchy tunes, beautiful people, and even

8

outrageous humor to grab our attention. If that fails, they scream at us. It is no coincidence that the volume goes up when the commercials come on! And it is no coincidence either that the mute button on many a remote control is worn down from overuse!

The ability to be attentive is a gift. Ask anyone with Attention Deficit Disorder (ADD). Or someone with a toothache. Or someone harboring resentment. But attentiveness is more than a gift; it is essential for salvation.

Jesus knew this. Although he may never have yelled "Pay attention!" he did say "Behold!" on a number of occasions. "Behold the lilies...behold this child...behold that poor widow putting in those two coins...behold, I make all things new." Jesus' "behold" was his way of saying, "Pay attention now! This is really important!" In fact, Jesus' entire life was bent on directing our attention, focusing our time and energy on the things that really matter in life: the love God has for us, the love we should have for each other, our personal relationship with God in prayer, and heeding the cry of the poor. In other words, the things necessary for salvation.

The devil, on the other hand, works very hard to draw our attention away from these things. Sometimes we imagine the devil's work consists of getting us to commit big sins—like cheating, lying, adultery, murder. But the devil's work isn't as difficult as that most of the time. Most of the time the devil is doing little more than diverting our attention from what really matters in life: the love God has for us, the love we should have for each other, our personal relationship with God in prayer, heeding the cry of the poor.

In my book *Everyday Epiphanies,* I wrote, "Love begins with noticing." Here I say, salvation begins with attentiveness to the things that really count. One of my favorite proverbs says it well: "The main thing is to keep the main thing the main thing!"

Who or what is getting my attention these days? Am I keeping the main thing the main thing in my life?

✚ God, help me to be attentive today to the things that really matter.

Availability

God does not ask for our ability or our inability, but for our availability.
—Anonymous

Years ago I took an Old Testament course with a professor who made the Scriptures come alive. I still remember the day he did a dramatic reading of the call of the prophet Isaiah (Isaiah 6:1–8). He explained that Isaiah was praying in the temple one day when he had a vision of God—complete with singing angels, a scary earthquake, and lots of billowing smoke. Realizing he had seen God, Isaiah was overwhelmed with the sense of his own sinfulness. As he cowered in a corner, one of the angels came to him and touched his lips with a burning coal, thus purifying him of his sin.

It was then that Isaiah overheard God talking to himself: "Whom shall I send to speak to my people? Who shall be my prophet?" After my professor spoke those words, he became Isaiah. Rising slowly from his desk, he pointed dramatically to his chest and cried out, "Here I am! Send me!" That image of Isaiah volunteering to be God's prophet has stayed with me all these years. It is a stunning example of availability.

Availability is the gift of the Spirit that enables us to offer ourselves to God. It means we place our time, talents, and energy at God's disposal. Availability is not easy. Why? First, when we volunteer ourselves to God, we never know what we're getting into. Availability is like handing God a blank check. We don't know what "amount" God is going to fill in. Little wonder we balk.

Another reason availability is hard is because we humans are very possessive by nature. This truth was brought home to me a while ago as I sat on the floor with my two-year-old grandnephew, Aaron. While playing with him, I happened to pick up his little rubber dinosaur. In a flash, Aaron grabbed the dinosaur from my hand, clutched it to his little chest, and cried, "MINE!" That's just how possessive we can be with our lives sometimes. When we sense God is asking us to do something, we clutch our time and talents to ourselves and cry, "Mine!" Hopefully, we (like

10

little Aaron) eventually learn that life (or a toy) is not something to cling to selfishly. It is a gift to share with others.

Availability is also difficult because it often involves changing our plans. And if there's one thing we like, it's making plans. It is fine to make plans, of course, as long as we remain open to change. Sometimes we are asked to change our plans in little ways. We were planning to go to a movie, for example, but our six-year-old comes down with a fever, so we stay home and care for her. Or we just sit down to watch TV when a friend calls who needs to talk, so we turn the TV off and listen to our friend for an hour. Other times availability will call us to modify our plans in big ways. We planned on having our Saturday mornings free, but we volunteer instead to teach third grade in the parish religious education program. Or we planned on having more time for ourselves once the kids were grown, but we find ourselves caring for an elderly parent instead. When Isaiah went to the temple that day, he wasn't planning on becoming a prophet. But he scrapped his own plans and made himself available to a God who needed him.

What can hinder availability to God? Fear can. Instead of saying, "Here I am, God!" we may say, "But I've never done anything like that before" or "I feel so inadequate to the task." At such times we should remember, if God is truly asking us to do this thing, then God will give us the graces we need to do it—or the graces we need to accept failure if we can't do it. Another thing that interferes with availability is our reluctance to let go of something we cherish. "But I had my heart set on doing *this*—not *that!*" we protest. At such times, it is good to recall that ultimately, there's only one thing worth setting our hearts on anyway: doing the will of God.

Jesus was totally available to God. In Gethsemane he said, "Not my will, but yours be done." In other words, "Here I am, God! Send me!"

How do I make myself available to God? What hinders me from greater availability?

✚ Here I am, God! Send me!

Beauty

Of all psychology's sins, the most mortal is its neglect of beauty.
—James Hillman

Two men who were old friends were walking down the road one evening when they began to argue with each other. As they went along, they began shouting at one another as each one tried to impose his view upon the other. Suddenly, one of them caught sight of the setting sun. At once he pointed it out to his friend. Immediately the two men ceased their arguing. Instead they stood side by side in silence, gazing in wonder and awe at the beauty of the sunset. After several minutes, when the sun had slipped beneath the horizon, the two friends started on their way again. Only now, having forgotten what they had been arguing about, they walked together cheerfully and at peace with one another.

This little story reminds us that beauty has the power to heal. Unfortunately, this healing power is not always recognized in our technological society. This fact is reflected even in the curricula of many of our schools. If educational budgets are cut, what goes first? Not science. Not math. Not even sports. No, the arts go first. Such thinking implies that the arts are dispensable. Beauty is something we can live without.

But is beauty dispensable? Thomas Moore, in his classic book, *Care of the Soul,* argues that beauty is absolutely essential for the health of the soul. In fact, he goes so far as to say that if we lack beauty in our lives, we will probably suffer from familiar disturbances such as depression, paranoia, meaninglessness, and addiction. Moore writes, "The soul craves beauty, and in its absence suffers what James Hillman has called 'beauty neurosis.'" The psychologist Carl Jung, also a believer in the power of beauty, once suggested to a colleague, "Why not go out into the forest for a time, literally? Sometimes a tree tells you more than you can read in books."

Christianity at its best has always understood and appreciated the power of beauty to nourish the soul. Just look at our ancient cathedrals with their stained glass windows and soaring spires, our solemn liturgies with their chants and incense. Just listen to the strains of Schubert's "Ave

Maria" or behold Michelangelo's *Pietà*. Just read the poetry of St. John of the Cross or the prose of St. Teresa of Avila. Beauty, says Christianity, has the power to bring people together, lift spirits, and inspire courage and sacrifice.

Jesus knew this. He was remarkably attentive to the beauty in his everyday life. He appreciated, for example, the beauty in nature. The gospels show him attuned to the weather patterns and changing seasons of his native place. He knew his trees, noticed flowers, and was even something of a bird watcher. Jesus also observed animals and often used them very effectively in his teachings. Who can forget that devoted mother hen gathering her chicks beneath her wings, that cunning fox retreating to his den, or that gangly camel trying to squeeze through that narrow gate?

Jesus appreciated beauty in other forms too. The son of a carpenter, he probably knew wood very well and had an eye for color, line, and texture. The son of a homemaker, he was well acquainted with the beauty of freshly baked bread, a carefully sewn garment, and good wine. As a devout Jew, he also knew the power of music and poetry. He loved stories so much, he made up some of his own that, to this day, rival some of the best ever told—for example, the parables of the Prodigal Son and the Good Samaritan.

But most of all, Jesus was attentive to the beauty of human love. He experienced love firsthand from his parents. Later he encountered it in the men and women who were so devoted to him. Throughout his ministry, Jesus marveled at the power of love to do incredibly beautiful things. Love could ingeniously lower a sick friend through the roof of a ceiling, give away one's whole sustenance at the temple treasury, and beg for a cure for a servant. Jesus' experience of human love made it easier for him to believe in the love that God, Abba, had for him.

Beauty is a gift of the Spirit that nourishes and heals our souls. This only makes sense, for ultimately, Beauty is but another name for God.

How do I make time for beauty in my life? Have I ever experienced beauty's healing power?

✠ Beauty, ever ancient and ever new, nourish and heal my soul today.

Bereavement

Those who live in the Lord never see each other for the last time.
—German proverb

The word "bereavement" means to be stripped, to be deprived of something usually through death. The word comes from the Old English words *be* and *reafian*, meaning "to be robbed." Grief is the emotional suffering that bereavement causes. If this is what bereavement and grief mean, then how in heaven's name can they be considered gifts of the Spirit? I will get to that. But first, here is what I know about bereavement and grief.

Bereavement cannot be measured. But we are forever trying to measure it. A friend of mine was burying her ninety-four-year-old father who had lived with her the last three years of his life. At the wake I overheard someone say to her, "But, Ruthie, you had him so long!"—implying that the pain of Ruth's grief should be lessened by that fact. Ruth's response was a good one. She cried, "I know, I know. But that's what makes this even harder, because every day he gave me another reason to love him!"

Who can measure the pain of bereavement? Who can compare one person's grief to another's? And yet we try always to make a comparison. We say things like, "But my husband was so young," as if losing an elderly husband is easier. Or "But he was my only son," as if losing one son when you have two is less painful. Or "She was taken from me so quickly," as if watching a loved one die slowly and painfully is much better. Or we try to convince ourselves that our grief isn't really that bad after all, thank you. We say foolish things like, "I know I'll get over this." Or "After all, I did have fifty-two years with her." Or "At least he's not suffering anymore." These are all attempts to reduce the agony, to diminish the pain. But they seldom work.

Grief is grief. It is not despair. It is not hunger. It is not paralysis. It is not fear. Although sometimes it can feel like all of these things, no, grief is grief. It is unlike anything else in the world.

We cannot run away from grief. We cannot say, "As long as I don't go near the hospital where he died, I'll be okay." Or "I'll stay away from the park where we used to walk, and I won't hurt so much." Or "I'll go to my sister's and get away from all this." No, grief will find you. No matter where you are. C. S. Lewis describes this so well in his poignant book, *A Grief Observed,* a journal he wrote after the death of his wife. He says that grief "is not local," that is, restricted to one place. No, he feels his wife's absence everywhere: "Her absence is like the sky, spread over everything."

Bereavement changes us. Once we have lost someone we love, we are never quite the same. After the death of her father, Anne Lamott, in her book *Operating Instructions,* writes this: "I don't think you really ever get over the death of the few people who matter most to you. It's too big. Oh, you do, the badly broken leg does heal, and you walk again, but always with a limp."

Death is not the only thing we grieve. Any loss can make us grieve: the loss of a job, a relationship, our hair, our eyesight, a cherished idea, a favorite place, an accustomed way of doing things, our youth. When we are grieving over the death of a loved one, people take notice, they understand. They go out of their way to offer their condolences. But when we are grieving things like the loss of a breast or our independence, sometimes we stand alone.

How is bereavement a gift of the Spirit? Because it is the underside of love, goodness, and meaning. We grieve because we have loved and have been loved. It is as simple as that. Perhaps there is no clearer proof of love's greatness than the pain we feel when the object of our love is taken from us. Grief also underscores the essential goodness and meaningfulness of life. If people were not good and things did not matter, we would never grieve. But people are good, things do count, and life does have meaning. That is grief's protest. That is also grief's promise.

What has been my experience with grief and bereavement?

✠ Jesus, Risen Lord, in my grieving I cling to your promise of everlasting love.

Childlikeness

*A teacher told the story of the Good Samaritan to her class and asked,
"What does this story teach you?" Said one child, "When I'm in trouble,
someone should help me!"*

The only appropriate way to begin a reflection on childlikeness is with children. Here are a few excerpts from the book *Children's Letters to God,* compiled by Stuart Hample and Eric Marshall:

Dear God, In Sunday school they told us what you do. Who does it when you are on vacation?   —Jane

Dear God, My grandpa says you were around when he was a little boy. How far back do you go?   —Love, Dennis

Dear God, I didn't think orange went with purple until I saw the sunset you made on Tuesday. That was *cool!*   —Eugene

When Jesus was asked to point to someone who epitomized the qualities he was looking for in his disciples, he didn't go to a palace, synagogue, or marketplace. No, he went to a playground. And there, calling over to himself a little girl with pigtails and freckles, he put his arm around her shoulders, and said to his disciples, *"This* is the kind of person I want you to become. *She* has the qualities I'm looking for!"

We can only begin to imagine the shock of his disciples as they sputtered, "Her?! A little kid?! This is a joke, right?" The disciples had every reason to be shocked. They protested, "But, Jesus, children are ignorant, immature, self-centered, undisciplined, helpless, naughty, naive, cruel, inconsiderate, and totally irresponsible. And they have no legal rights whatsoever." In short, children were all those things the disciples, as adults, were trying so hard not to be.

Jesus probably agreed with their appraisal of children. Although he didn't have any children of his own, he had been around them enough to abandon all romantic notions he may have had about them. Besides, he knew firsthand just how naughty and inconsiderate a child could be. Hadn't he, at age twelve (an age when he should have known better), run away for three days from his parents? What grief he had caused them! He remembered the scolding they gave him too, right there in the temple. It was a scolding he certainly deserved.

But Jesus did not retract what he said. He didn't say, "Yeah, Yeah, it was a joke. Gotcha, didn't I?" No, he was insistent and made his point even more plain: "I'm telling you, you will *not* enter the Kingdom of Heaven *unless you become like this little kid!*"

We might ask, what is it about children that make them shoo-ins for the Kingdom of God? Here and in other passages, Jesus tells us. For one thing, children are open. They let reality in—not like so many adults who, over the years, build elaborate barriers to shield themselves against the real world. Those barriers, unfortunately, keep out not only the world, they keep out God too who can come into our lives only through that real world.

Children are trustful too. They readily take your hand. They go where you lead them. They believe what you tell them. Isn't this receptivity exactly what we need in our relationship with God? Don't we have to trust God, take God's hand, go where God may lead us, and believe what God tells us?

And finally, children have no real claims on their parents' love. They do nothing to merit or earn the love that is poured out upon them from the moment they enter the world. Good parents don't love their kids because they *have to.* They love their kids because they love their kids. There's no other way to say it. The gratuitous love of a parent for a child is a heck of a lot like God's love for us.

How childlike am I? Who am I loving gratuitously?

✚ God, you who are Father, you who are Mother, give me the heart of a child!

Commitment

"Make of your life something beautiful for God."

My parents have been married for sixty-one years. Sometimes my father teases my mother by saying, "Remember, Mil, I signed the marriage license in pencil! I can still change my mind!"

Making a commitment means signing your name in ink. It means giving your word and meaning it. It means promising something today that has ramifications for tomorrow. Every commitment involves some kind of a loss. If I make a commitment to lose twenty pounds, I cannot eat everything I might want to eat. If I make a commitment to marry Patti, I will not be marrying Laura, Allison, or Veronica. If I make a commitment to become a nun, I cannot get married too. But every commitment also involves a gain: I will lose twenty pounds, I will marry Patti, I will be a nun. The only reason we make a commitment is because we believe the gain far outweighs the loss. The day we no longer believe that is probably the day we question or end our commitment.

Some commitments are more important than others. Once, at fifteen, I was at a wedding when I sensed a young man was about to ask me to dance. Since he was much older and a little shorter than I was, I did *not* want to dance with him. Panicking as he approached, I whispered to a married cousin, "I *won't* dance with him! I'd rather die first!" She calmly replied, "Melannie, he's asking you to *dance* with him—not to *marry* him!" It is very important to distinguish between major commitments and minor ones. (By the way, I *did* dance with that young man. But I did not marry him!)

Everyone makes commitments. Even selfish people do. They make a commitment to live for themselves. Some people say they never make any commitments. But even that is a commitment. Why do we make commitments? To channel our energies (see the chapter on DISCIPLINE), to give our lives direction, and to help ourselves do those things we see as good, meaningful, and beautiful.

Jesus made a commitment. One day he told his disciples what his commitment was: "My food is to do the will of him who sent me" (John

4:34). In other words, "My essential commitment in life is to do God's will." Keeping that commitment was not easy for Jesus. During his forty days in the wilderness, for example, he was tempted by Satan to break his commitment not once, but three times. Throughout his public life, Jesus' enemies also tried to thwart his resolve with a variety of tactics: argumentation, mockery, threats. Even his closest friend Peter tried to dissuade him from keeping a commitment that was taking him to Jerusalem to die. But Jesus held fast. In Gethsemane, he reconfirms his commitment when he says to Abba, "Take this cup away from me, but not what I will but what you will" (Mark 14:36).

Jesus called his followers to make a commitment to him: "Come follow me" (Mark 1:17). It is a commitment that has to be wholehearted: "When a (merchant) finds a pearl of great price, he sells all that he has and buys it" (Matthew 13:46). It must be irrevocable: "No one who sets a hand to the plow and looks back to what was left behind is fit for the kingdom of God" (Luke 9:62). The commitment to Jesus takes precedence over all other commitments, even those to one's family. It is a commitment that will not be easy: "I am sending you like lambs in the midst of wolves" (Luke 10:1–12), and "Whoever does not carry his own cross and come after me cannot be my disciple" (Luke 14:27). But Jesus also assured his followers that he himself would give them the strength necessary to live out their commitment to him: "And behold, I am with you always, until the end of the age" (Matthew 28:20).

For us Christians, then, there is ultimately only one commitment. It is the same commitment that Jesus made: *to do the will of God.* It is a commitment we will be tempted to live halfheartedly at times or even abandon altogether. It is one that constantly challenges us to discern God's will in our everyday lives (see the chapter on COUNSEL). But if we, like Jesus, hold fast to this commitment to the end, our joy will know no bounds (John 16:24).

How strong is my commitment to Jesus? How are my other commitments helping me to keep this essential one?

✚ Jesus, help me to live my commitments today with greater trust in your strength.

Common Sense

It is right and fitting, I believe, to go mad over the fair Messiah. A great wisdom it is, indeed, to go mad, out of one's mind with the love of God.
—Blessed Jacopone da Todi

I was going to call this next gift "prudence," but I decided to go with "common sense" instead. To me, they both mean essentially the same thing. Personally, however, "prudence" has a negative connotation for me that I cannot shake. Maybe that is because in my early days in the convent, if someone said to me, "Now, Melannie, be prudent!" it meant only one thing: "Now, Melannie, don't you *dare* do what you're thinking of doing!" Prudence to me is so cautionary. It is the proverbial wet blanket and killjoy. Even the sound of the word turns me off. Try this in the privacy of your bathroom. Stand before the mirror and say "prudence" very slowly and see what happens to your face. See how that first syllable "pru" puckers your lips and crinkles your nose? That is another reason I called this chapter "common sense."

What exactly is common sense? It is hard to define. I was tempted to say that common sense tells you what common sense is, but that's not fair. So, even though I am not going to define common sense, I will describe some of its characteristics. First, common sense is not something we are born with; it is something we garner along the road of life. A newborn baby, for example, has no common sense whatsoever—except that it cries and sucks. But those are instincts, not common sense (see the chapter on INSTINCT). No, common sense comes with experience. We adults know that we do not run across a street without looking both ways. That's common sense. But a four-year-old doesn't know that. And even a nine-year-old who may know it, can, tragically, forget it when her ball rolls into the street. So there are degrees of common sense.

I am not implying, of course, that everyone gets more common sense the older they get. Heavens, no! I know adults with little common sense and teenagers with a lot of it. Nor do individuals have equal amounts of common sense about all aspects of their life. No, a man might have much common sense about the stock market, for example, and no common sense when it comes to relationships.

Another characteristic of common sense is that it is unreflective. If I follow my common sense I do not take a lot of time thinking about what to do. My common sense tells me almost instantly. If I am bathing the baby and the phone rings, I do not have to ask myself, "What should I do? a) Leave the baby in the tub and go answer the phone? b) Snatch the baby out, wrap her in a towel, and run to the phone? Or c) Ignore the phone and finish bathing the baby?" Common sense would immediately tell me: c. Unreflectively.

The paradox is, however, that although common sense is unreflective, the only way we get more of it is through reflection. This means, we periodically pause and take stock of the choices our common sense has been telling us to make in order to see where those choices are leading us and what they may be teaching us.

Jesus advocated common sense. He said, "If your child asks you for an egg, would you hand him a scorpion?" (Luke 11:12). No, that's not common sense! "If you set about building a house, would you build it on sand?" (Matthew 7:26–27). No, that's foolish! Jesus was implying that a lot of things that are common sense in our natural, everyday lives, are common sense for our spiritual lives as well.

Just one more thing: common sense, like his sister prudence, can be an old stick in the mud at times—especially when it comes to religious matters (see the chapter on DARING). Jesus knew this too. That man who sold everything to buy that unpromising looking field looked like he had no common sense—at least to his neighbors. That's because they did not know about the hidden treasure! But he did! And, as Jesus says, if you find such a treasure, the only thing to do is risk all for it! That is *real* common sense!

Where is my common sense taking me these days? Has my love for Jesus ever made me do things that do not look like common sense?

✚ Jesus, you are my treasure! Following you makes all the sense in the world!

Companionship

Above all else, it seems to me,
You need some jolly company
To see life can be fun.
—Goethe

The director of a hospice in Detroit was explaining his volunteer program to me. He said, "We've learned that pain comes in many forms. One major form of pain is loneliness." He gave me an example. One of their clients loved to play chess. But his illness prevented him from going out and finding someone to play chess with. The hospice found a volunteer who also liked to play chess. Said the director, "That volunteer now goes every week to play chess with that man." Then he added, "You know, one of the most important services our volunteers provide is companionship."

Companionship is a word rich with Eucharistic overtones. The word comes from the Latin *companio,* which literally means "one who breaks bread with another." (*Com* means "with" and *panis* means "bread"). Companionship began in the garden of Eden. In the second creation account (Genesis 2:4–25), God creates Adam first and places him in the lush garden God has prepared for him. Adam has everything a man could want: loads of food, gorgeous scenery, unheard of freedom, no boss, no deadlines, and tons of leisure time. But God detects that something is wrong. Maybe God saw Adam hanging his head and dragging his feet as he walked through the garden. Or perhaps Adam was beginning to talk to himself. Whatever abnormal behavior he was exhibiting, God spots it and diagnoses the problem: "It is not good for man to be alone," and comes up with a solution: "I will make a suitable partner for him."

So God creates the animals—cats, dogs, pelicans, zebras, rhinos, dolphins, two-toed sloths—but even these animals do not alleviate Adam's loneliness. That's when God comes up with an even better idea. (There are some of us who maintain that this particular idea represents the high point of creation!) God creates woman! Eve, then, is the first-ever companion.

There are some who would trace companionship back even further than the Garden of Eden—all the way back to God. I am reminded of that magnificent poem called "Creation" by the African-American poet, James Weldon Johnson. In the poem, Johnson attributes creation itself to God's need for companionship. The poem shows God stepping out into space and confessing, "I'm lonely." To ease his loneliness, God decides to "make me a world." The poem shows God fashioning the universe one day at a time. After each day's labor, God pronounces the work good, but then adds, "I'm lonely still." Eventually God creates Adam and Eve. By doing so, God's loneliness is eased, for God has found suitable companions with whom to share both life and love.

When Jesus begins his public ministry, one of the first things he does is to find companions, those individuals who will share his life and ministry in a special way. Whenever Jesus faces a difficult situation, he gathers these companions around himself—sometimes all twelve, sometimes only a few. Jesus Christ, the Son of God, the Savior of the world, needed the companionship of others. Even he, as strong and powerful and good as he was, couldn't go it alone.

We can't go it alone either. We cannot face the challenges of life without the support of others. This need for companionship is one we must never be ashamed of. We must never think, "If I were more mature, I could stand on my own two feet." Or, "If my faith were stronger, I wouldn't have to rely so much on others." No, our need for companionship, fellowship, friendship, is in the very fabric of our human psyche. It is yet one more way that we are made in the image and likeness of God.

Who accompanies me along my spiritual pathway? For whom do I provide companionship?

✠ God, my loving companion, thank you for all those people you have given me to share my life and love.

Compassion

Whatever God does, the first outburst is always compassion.
—Meister Eckhart

One of the best things Christianity has going for it is its identification with compassion. Throughout history, the Church—at its best—has been legendary for reaching out with compassion to the poor. The very concept of a hospital, for example, is solidly rooted in Christian compassion. Even in our own day, individuals like Dorothy Day, Frances Cabrini, John Bosco, Mother Teresa, and Henri Nouwen are known primarily for their compassion toward those in need.

Conversely, the Church, at its worst, is notorious for its lack of compassion. Stories abound of so-called Christians who turned away the needy, exploited the poor, and even slaughtered the innocent. Such accounts are scandalous precisely because they go against compassion, the hallmark of Christianity, the hallmark of Jesus himself.

Jesus was compassionate. This is the message that hits us squarely between the eyes whenever we stroll through the gospels. There's Jesus healing the sick, giving bread to the hungry, teaching the confused, consoling the bereaved, challenging the status quo, encouraging the downcast, embracing a little child, sobbing over the death of a friend, and (perhaps most compassionately of all) forgiving the very people who tortured and executed him. Our final destiny, says Jesus in his parables, is ultimately determined by our compassion—not our humility, austerity, honesty, prayerfulness, orthodoxy, or purity. In the end, it is compassion—or the lack of it—that will separate the sheep from the goats, the saved from the unsaved.

The word "compassion," though, is easily misunderstood or misconstrued. Perhaps that is why Jesus is so absolutely clear what he means by the word. In the parable of the Last Judgment (Matthew 25:31–46), he gives example after example of not merely what compassion *is*, but what it *does*. Compassion feeds the hungry, gives drink to the thirsty, welcomes the stranger, clothes the naked, cares for the ill, and visits the imprisoned. And just to be sure we have heard what he said, Jesus repeats all six examples again at the end of the parable. If we want a gauge for our compassion, this parable provides a fine one.

Compassion knows no age either. We do not have to be twenty-one to be compassionate. Even little children can begin to learn compassion— and should. Recently I read about a ten-year-old girl with long blonde hair that hung all the way down to her waist. She was proud of her hair— and justifiably so. But then she heard about an organization that collects human hair to make wigs for people undergoing chemotherapy. What did that little girl do? That's right. She got her hair cut and donated it to that organization. When I saw the picture of her holding her twelve-inch braid and smiling, I thought, "Now that's compassion!"

Just as we are never too young to start being compassionate, we are never too old to be compassionate, either. I am continuously edified by the elderly sisters in our health care facility who crochet baby clothes for organizations such as Birthright, clip postage stamps for the missions, or help each other shuffle down the hall. Compassion knows no gender, either. Men are called to be compassionate just as women are. Masculinity in no way precludes compassion. Compassion knows no certain economic status, no single career, no particular location, no specific language. In short, compassion knows no excuses.

In addition, we must never confuse compassion with things that may look like compassion, but are not. For example, compassion is not sympathy. Sympathy says, "You poor thing!" Compassion goes beyond sympathy and says, "I am deeply moved by your plight. How may I help you?" Compassion is not obsequiousness. It never says, "If I help you, what will you do for me?"

And finally, we must remember that compassion is a privilege. Jesus reveals himself as the compassionate one not simply because he does good works for you and me, but also because he also allows us the privilege of doing good works for and through him.

What are some of the concrete ways I express my compassion for others?

✚ Jesus, Compassionate One, thank you for working through me today.

Counsel

Discernment is the meeting point of prayer and action.
—Thomas H. Green, SJ

The year was 1960. John F. Kennedy and Richard M. Nixon were in a tight race for the presidency. A certain nun in Cleveland couldn't decide which candidate to vote for. In desperation, she took out her Bible and prayed, "Lord, give me a sign!" Closing her eyes, she opened the Bible at random and pointed her finger to the page. Opening her eyes, she read in amazement the words her finger was pointing to: "His name is John" (Luke 1:63).

Whether this story is true or not, I don't know. If it is, Kennedy certainly had the advantage, for the name John shows up many times in Scripture, whereas the name Richard doesn't appear even once! But the truth is, there are better ways to seek God's advice than randomly opening the Bible and pointing to a verse. The gift of the Spirit that puts us in touch with those better ways is the gift of counsel.

In his book, *Surprised by the Spirit,* Father Edward Farrell notes that the gift of counsel is one of the more elusive gifts of the Spirit. He suggests, therefore, (and I agree with him) that it might be better to think of counsel in terms of discernment. What is meant by discernment? Simply put, discernment is the quest to know God's will. Over the centuries, many books have been written about discernment. In this chapter, I will simply share a few thoughts on discernment that I have "discerned" over the years—from reading as well as from my own experience.

First of all, discernment is absolutely essential for our spiritual lives. One reason is because the will of God is not always obvious. Another is the fact that there are other spirits (both in ourselves and in the world around us) besides God's Spirit that can influence our choices. Most of us learned quickly in life that every movement of our hearts does not come from God. Some movements proceed from other spirits such as selfishness ("But I want *this!*") or fear ("I'm afraid to do *that!*") or laziness ("I wanna stay put!"). Similarly, every piece of advice we are exposed to on a given day does not proceed from the Spirit of God.

Some advice, in fact, is diametrically opposed to God's Spirit. Our culture, for example, may tell us to think only of ourselves, to amass as many material goods as we can, or to lie if it helps us to get ahead. The gift of discernment helps us to sort out these many messages in order to detect God's voice among the cacophony.

Good discernment is rooted in the conviction that we are loved by God. Anything that makes us doubt this fundamental truth is not from God. At the same time, discernment reminds us that we are sinners. This knowledge of our failings, rather than depressing us, only makes us more appreciative of God's mercy and more understanding of and compassionate toward others. Good discernment also calls us toward ever greater selflessness. It always asks, "Will this make me a more loving person?"

Discernment does not seek God's will in the abstract: "What is God's will for humankind?" Rather, it seeks God's will in the concrete: "What is God's will for me in these particular circumstances?" Discernment, however, goes beyond asking, "What does God want me to do here?" Ultimately it asks, "Who is God calling me to become?" In addition, discernment is not always individual. It can also be communal: "Who is God calling *us* to become?"

In his book on discernment, *Weeds Among the Wheat*, Thomas Green, SJ, says that good discernment presupposes three things: that we have the desire to do God's will (Green calls this desire "a committed faith"); that we have an openness to God's will (in other words, if we are wedded to our own will, discernment is impossible); and discernment presupposes we have knowledge of God (see the chapter on INTIMACY). If we don't know God personally through an ardent prayer life, how can we know what pleases God? For more serious discerning, it is often wise to seek the help of a good friend or spiritual director, someone (of course) who is familiar with the ways of God.

And finally, Green says, "Discernment, like prayer, is an art. It is learned by doing, not just by reading about it."

How do I discern God's will in my own life? What factors help or hinder good discernment for me?

✝ Spirit of Counsel, give me a discerning heart!

Daring

The greatest hazard in life is to risk nothing.
—Anonymous

A preacher said to a friend, "We have just had the greatest revival our church has ever experienced." The friend asked, "How many did you add to your church membership?" Said the preacher, "None. We lost five hundred!"

The little story makes a good point. How challenging is our Christian faith? Does our faith merely provide comfort and consolation for us in times of trouble, or does it continuously challenge us to become better persons, to grow in sensitivity, and to broaden the scope of our love? One suspects that if preachers really dared their congregations to live the Christian faith more authentically, many churches would experience a drastic decline in membership!

But the fact remains, Jesus was a daring person. He dared to forsake the security and obscurity of an ordinary life in Nazareth, for example, and chose instead the life of an itinerant preacher, a life fraught with vulnerability and danger. When he started his preaching ministry and began to gain some notoriety, his relatives and hometown friends became embarrassed by his behavior. They tried to convince Jesus to forget this preaching life, to come back home, and to settle down. When they saw he wasn't listening to reason, they tried force. But Jesus faced the challenge of their rationality and eluded their grasp.

Not only was Jesus himself daring, he dared others as well. When he was recruiting disciples, he did not pull any punches. He was ruthlessly honest with his followers, explaining in graphic detail what discipleship with him would entail. It would demand renunciation: "Foxes have dens and birds of the sky have nests, but the Son of Man has nowhere to rest his head" (Matthew 8:20). It would invite ridicule and persecution: They will "insult you and persecute you and utter every kind of evil against you" (Matthew 5:11). And it could even lead to death: "If these things are done when the wood is green, what will happen when it is dry?" (Luke 23:31).

28

Jesus never pretended that discipleship with him would be easy. He knew he was demanding of his followers a moral standard of living heretofore unseen by them. The disciples were shocked on a regular basis by many of the things Jesus said. They openly questioned his words about forgiveness, monogamy, and universal love, for example, with the hope that maybe they had heard him wrong. "You mean we've got to forgive more than once?...You mean we can have only one wife?...You mean we've got to love *them?*" And Jesus never backed down or took back what he said either. On the contrary, one day he even let a stellar candidate go rather than lower his standards of discipleship.

Being a Christian is tough. If we think otherwise, we are not living authentic Christianity. If we imagine, for example, that we are finally finished with forgiving, we are wrong. If we think we have shared more than enough with the poor, we are wrong. If we think we have successfully cleared the high bar of Christian love, then the bar is too low. Christianity is tough. In fact, left to our own resources, it is downright impossible. As Jesus himself told us, we can become his followers only through the generosity and power of the Holy Spirit.

By listing "daring" as a gift of the Spirit, I am not saying that caution does not have a place in our lives. Of course it does. But I am suggesting that perhaps we allow caution too much sway in our decision making—as individuals, parishes, local communities, and church. By saying things like "But we've never done that before" or "What will others think?" we cramp the Spirit's style and lessen the Spirit's effectiveness. Perhaps it would be better to raise questions like these instead: "What is something worthwhile that we have never dared to do before?...How different would my datebook look if I were more daring like Jesus?"

Once when I was on retreat, I found myself writing this short prayer in my journal, "God, help me to love you less cautiously." It is a prayer I still dare to say on a regular basis.

Do I find Christianity easy or tough? How daring am I when it comes to my faith?

✠ Daring Spirit, help me to take some Christlike risks today.

Dazzlement

Lord, you are like a wildflower. You spring up in places where we least expect you. The bright color of your grace dazzles us.
—Henry Suso

Several years before he died in 1972, Rabbi Abraham Heschel suffered a heart attack from which he never fully recovered. Samuel Dresner, a friend and a fellow rabbi, came to see Heschel in his New York apartment. Heschel, who could speak only in a whisper, told Dresner that when he first regained consciousness after his heart attack, his first feelings were not despair or anger. "I felt only gratitude to God for my life, for every moment I had lived," he said. "I was ready to depart. 'Take me, O Lord,' I thought, 'I have seen so many miracles.'"

Heschel was a man filled with a sense of wonder. In fact, in the preface to his book of Yiddish poems, he wrote this short prayer: "I did not ask for success; I asked for wonder. And you gave it to me." In the Bible, this sense of wonder is sometimes called "fear of the Lord." Now when we hear the word "fear," we picture someone running away from a wasp or a hornet. But the phrase "fear of the Lord" has nothing to do with fright. Rather, the Hebrew word *yir'ah* is best translated not as "fear," but as "awe" or "respect." In this chapter, I'm calling "fear of the Lord" the gift of dazzlement.

The Bible is filled with stories of individuals who were dazzled by the living God. Moses was dazzled by God in a burning bush (Exodus 3), the prophet Elijah in a gentle breeze or (as one translation puts it) in the "sound of sheer silence" (1 Kings 19:12). At the birth and naming of John the Baptist, when the mute Zechariah was suddenly able to speak again, his friends were dazzled: "Then fear came upon all their neighbors" (Luke 1:65). When Jesus calmed the raging storm at sea, the apostles "were afraid and amazed, and said to one another, 'Who is this who commands even the winds and the sea, and they obey him?'" (Luke 8:25). And after Jesus' ascension, when the apostles themselves worked many wonders, the crowds were rightfully amazed: "Awe came upon everyone" (Acts 2:43).

There is a paradox operating here. Because believers *fear* the Lord, they need *not fear* anything or anyone else. Abraham was told not to fear, for God was his shield (Genesis 15:1). Similarly, Isaac was told by God to have no fear "since I am with you" (Genesis 26:24). As the Israelites stood trembling in their sandals at the edge of the Red Sea, Moses cried out to them, "Fear not! Stand your ground, and you will see the victory the Lord will win for you today" (Exodus 14:13). The people did as Moses directed, and God dazzled them by splitting the Red Sea in two.

The New Testament also counsels people not to fear. Gabriel told Mary not to fear for she had found favor with God (Luke 1:30). The angel also counseled Joseph not to be afraid to take Mary as his wife even though her child was not his (Matthew 1:20). In Bethlehem, the angel assuaged the shepherds' fear with, "Do not be afraid; for behold, I bring to you good news of great joy" (Luke 2:10). And Jesus, on numerous occasions, said to individuals, "Fear not...fear not...fear not." The Bible is clear. God is in charge. (Isn't that amazing?) There is no need to be anxious. (How wonder-full!) No matter what happens. (Wow!)

Matthias Newman, OSB, in an article entitled "The Burning Bush: A Meditation on Wonder" (*Praying,* Nov–Dec '96), defines wonder as "a total attitude of life that recognizes a marvelous dimension to all existence, delights in it, and is open to its recreative power." I like the phrase "a marvelous dimension to all existence." That means anything possesses the potential to dazzle us with its recreative power: a daffodil bobbing, an owl hooting, the scent of pine, the kindness of a stranger, the embrace of a friend. For all existence has the power to put us in touch with our incredibly marvelous, amazingly wonderful God.

In a piece entitled "Wonder, Yogi, Gladly" (*The Other Side,* Nov–Dec. '97), David James Duncan writes, "Wonder may be the feel of truth touching our very skin." Maybe dazzlement is the feel of Truth touching our very heart.

Have I been dazzled by God lately? What can get in the way of wonder?

✝ God, make me more open to the dazzlement of your love.

Desire

Jesus asked, "What are you looking for?"
—John 1:38

We come into the world with desires. At first they are quite simple: milk, warmth, a clean diaper, a rattle, a little bit of cuddling. But soon our desires grow. We desire not merely milk, but chocolate chip cookies, pizza, and French fries. We want not merely a rattle, but another stuffed animal to go with the dozen we already have. And we want Mommy's attention right away—and Daddy's and Grandma's and the teacher's. With the onset of adolescence, our desires become deeper and more intense. We desire acceptance, friendship, intimacy, sex. As adults, our desires increase even more: we want a good family, a nice home, meaningful employment, job security, peace of mind, a sense of fulfillment.

As Christians, some of us were taught to mistrust our desires. We were led to believe that all our desires were basically selfish or tainted. The whole concept of concupiscence was boiled down to this: "If you desire it, it must be bad. In fact, the more intensely you desire it, the worse it is!" We were told that happiness was found in denying our desires. In fact, we should really desire only one thing: to do God's will. We were seldom taught that we might discover God's will precisely by following our desires—to their deepest roots.

But that is what Jesus taught about desires. One day, John the Baptist was preaching his stuff to the crowds when Jesus happened to walk by (John 1:35–42). Seeing Jesus, John pointed to him and said, "Behold, the Lamb of God." Some of John's disciples, hearing what he had said, began to follow Jesus—probably not too closely. Jesus, aware that they were tailing him, turned around and asked them, "What are you looking for?" That question may very well be one of the most important questions in the Gospel. For what Jesus was really asking was: "What do you want?" or "What is it you desire?"

The disciples were caught off guard by Jesus' question. So flustered were they, they gave a pretty dumb answer: "Master, where are you staying?" Jesus realized the inanity of their response, but he played right along and said, "Come and see." The disciples followed Jesus, saw where he was staying, and ended up spending the rest of the day with him. Their discipleship with Christ began by answering the question, "What are you looking for? What is it you desire?"

That was not the only occasion when Jesus led individuals to get in touch with their desires. To several sick people who approached him for a cure, Jesus asked, "What is it that you want?" or "What do you want me to do?" He never presumed to know what was inside another person's heart. He asked. By doing so, he helped people to discover and name their deepest desires for themselves.

Jesus himself was in touch with his own desires. And on several occasions he even shared these desires with his disciples. Once he said, "My food is to do the will of him who sent me" (John 4:34). At the Last Supper, he told his disciples, "I have eagerly desired to eat this Passover with you before I suffer" (Luke 22:15).

A good way to begin praying, then, is to ask ourselves the same question Jesus asked his first disciples, "What am I looking for?" That question can take a variety of forms: "What am I desiring right now?... What would I like to see happen today?... What do I want from this day?... What do I desire for my life?" As we ask ourselves this question, we must not be in too much of a hurry to answer it. Answering it may take some time. In fact, we must even be ready to admit, "I don't know what I want." It can take a while to get down to the deepest desires of our heart. A quick response, on the other hand, may be expressing only a surface desire: a new car, more money, peace and quite, more time. But if we trace the root of these surface desires, we just might get in touch with some of our deeper longings: companionship, security, meaning, truth, love.

But I've saved the best news for last. All our desires will eventually lead to God. In other words, God is the fulfillment of all our longing. What's more, God desires, too. God desires us! In fact, God desires us far more than we desire God. In that fact is our hope and salvation!

What am I looking for? If I really believed God desires me more than I desire God, what impact would that have on my life?

✛ God of my longing, increase my desire for you!

Discipline

The only authentic discipleship is a life of love lived unpretentiously for others out of a life lived for God.
—Brennan Manning

One day when I was about four, I crawled up onto the piano bench and began to fiddle with the keys. I was looking for "Jingle Bells." I knew it was in the keys—somewhere—because I had heard my mother and older sister playing it. I hit a key. Then another. And another. After much stopping and starting and stopping and starting, I finally found "Jingle Bells." The whole song! Heartened by my success, I began searching for other songs among the keys. Over time I found them, too: "Home on the Range," "It's Howdy Doody Time," and even "The Blue Skirt Waltz."

I thought I was ready to take piano lessons like my older sister, but I was told I had to wait until second grade. By the time I finally got that old, I was raring to go. With three years of playing by ear to my credit, I thought learning to play for real would be easy and fun. But I was wrong. For suddenly I was initiated into the harsh world of piano lessons.

First, I had to learn to read music. This meant staring for hours at flash cards, trying to distinguish between an F and an A, a G and an E. This seemed too much like work to me. In addition, I could no longer play just the songs I wanted to play. I now had to play the songs my piano teacher told me to play. And, quite frankly, I did not like some of those songs. And finally, I now had to practice. This meant I no longer played just when I felt like it; I had to play nearly every day—even when there were other things I preferred to do like ride my bike or play with the cat.

My experience with piano lessons taught me a lot about discipline. It also taught me a lot about discipleship. For the two words, "discipline" and "discipleship" are first cousins. To put it simply, it takes discipline to be a good disciple. What exactly is discipline? I see discipline as a channeling of energies. A good image of discipline for me has always been a rocket blasting off. The blast of any rocket is really a massive explosion—a massive channeled explosion. The energy of the blast is channeled to propel the rocket in a single direction, carrying it to its destination.

Being a disciple of Jesus is also all about the channeling of energy in a single direction. On numerous occasions and in a variety of images Jesus warns us that being his disciple requires discipline. "No one can serve two masters," he says in Matthew 6:24. In other words, our service must be channeled in one direction. Another time he says, "No one who sets a hand to the plow and looks to what was left behind is fit for the kingdom of God" (Luke 9:62). Our attention, our energy, must not be diverted. And again, Jesus says, "Carry no money bag, no sack, no sandals" (Luke 10:4). Money bags and sandals are things that could weigh us down, thus reducing the force of our energy.

The primary energy we have, of course, is love. Discipline, then, is what enables us to live a life of love—which (of course) is precisely what discipleship means. Sometimes loving is easy. We can love when we want, whom we want, and on our own terms. But sooner or later, love will become more arduous. We will be called to love in ways we find difficult or nearly impossible. We will be asked to love some individuals we find unattractive, ornery, hurtful, or immoral. We will be invited to love on God's terms and not our own. And that is precisely what discipleship with Jesus means.

P.S. I took piano lessons for six years. To this day, I still like to sit down at a piano and plunk out not just "Jingle Bells," but things like "Moon River" and "Tchaikovsky's Piano Concerto No. 1." I never became a virtuoso, true, but I am very glad I had the discipline to stick with the lessons, for I still get a kick out of finding songs hidden in those keys!

What does discipline mean for me? How does my discipleship with Jesus channel my love?

✞ Jesus, help me to live a life for others out of my love for you.

Diversity

Diversity is not the enemy of unity. The enemy of unity is
hatred or simply the lack of love.
—Demetrius Dumm, OSB

I saw a cartoon recently that showed a group of high school students walking out of school. They were all dressed identically: same baggy jeans,
same T-shirts, same baseball caps on backwards, same sneakers. One says,
"I heard we're gonna have to wear uniforms in school next year." Another
complains, "That's not fair! I don't wanna dress like everybody else!"

Many of us have a peculiar relationship with the concept of diversity.
In one way we are all for it. "I wanna do my own thing! I have to express
my individuality! I'm different from you and that's great!" But in another way, we mistrust it. "Diversity will destroy community! We have to
do things alike! In unity is our strength!" The teens in the cartoon wanted diversity in dress, yet they all wore the exact same outfit. Sometimes
we do something similar. We say we are all for diversity, yet we squelch
any sign of it in ourselves and in others.

Why can we be so intolerant of diversity? For one thing, we may be
afraid. Afraid of what? You name it! We are afraid of germs, wasps,
snakes, lightning, strangers, heights, new ideas, the future, God, and
even ourselves. This innate fear causes us to do some strange things—for
example, to curb diversity. We reason, the more diversity there is, the less
we will know and understand. The less we know and understand, the
less control we will have over our life. And that's scary. That's bad.

We can curb diversity in small ways. We can demand that everyone
act in the same way. We can say things like this: "We should all dress
alike...We should all pray alike....We should all hold the same values."
People who are intolerant of diversity usually assume (mistakenly) that
there is really only one right way of doing things, one right way of being
in the world. And it's their way (of course!).

But diversity is not a threat. It is a gift. In fact, it is one of the out-
standing characteristics of God's creation. All we have to do is look at

the world of plants and animals. When God thought "flower," God did not think merely daisy or rose. God thought lily, violet, geranium, orchid, hydrangea, daffodil, iris, jack-in-the-pulpit, pansy, aster, azalea, foxglove, lady's-slipper, and so on. Similarly, when God conceived "animal," God did not stop with dog or cat, but continued on with horse, goat, whale, camel, parrot, cobra, rabbit, possum, lion, elephant, whale, giraffe, aardvark, hedgehog, etc. And when God thought "people," God did not stop with Adam and Eve, but continued with Enos, Abraham, Sarah, Isaac, Moses, Judith, Ruth, David, Hector, Ammad, Kim, Carmelita, and even us.

St. Paul, in his first letter to the Corinthians, makes it clear that diversity is not only a characteristic of creation, it is also a characteristic of the Spirit. He writes: "There are different kinds of spiritual gifts but the same Spirit; there are different forms of service but the same Lord; there are different workings but the same God who produces all of them in everyone" (1 Corinthians 12:4–6). Paul sees the diversity among Christians as a reflection of the diversity among the Persons of the Blessed Trinity. In the passage quoted, the Spirit is the Holy Spirit, the Lord is Jesus, and God is the Father or Creator. God is diversity. The three Persons are unique from each other. We who have been fashioned in God's image, share in God's innate diversity. Diversity, like all of God's creation, is essentially good.

Anthony de Mello, SJ, tells a fanciful little story that seems appropriate here. When God created the world, God smiled and said, "That's good!" But the devil also looked upon what God had made, and he smiled too and said, "That's good!" Only he added, "Now let's organize it!"

We might ask ourselves these questions today. How welcoming am I of diversity whenever I encounter it—especially in other people? Do I see diversity as delightful or lamentable? Do I fear and resent what is different or unfamiliar, or do I see it as fascinating and challenging?

What have been some of my experiences of diversity—especially in people? Do I see diversity as a blessing, a challenge, or both?

✚ God of diversity, help me to appreciate and delight in what is different and unfamiliar.

Failure

Mistakes are the usual bridge between inexperience and wisdom.
—Phyllis Theroux

The other day I was driving down a side street through a small industrial park. Up ahead, I spotted a huge semi in the road. As I got closer, I saw that the driver was trying to back his truck into the driveway of a small company. Since he was blocking the street, I had no choice but to stop and watch. I was amazed. Here was a man trying to get a truck as big as the Queen Mary into a space the size of my broom closet! My first reaction was, "You'll never do it, Buddy!" But as I watched him, my "You'll never do it, Buddy!" gradually became a "You can do it, Buddy!" as I began cheering for the guy. Within a few minutes, after some very careful maneuvering, the man accomplished his goal. He parked his truck in that narrow driveway. (When he was through, I almost jumped out of my car, clapped my hands and yelled, "Bravo, Buddy! Well done!" But there were cars behind me and their drivers, no doubt, would have thought me very strange!)

I bet if I asked the man, "How'd you learn to do that?" he would say something like, "I've had lots of practice." And if he got really honest with me, he might even say, "You should've seen the first dozen times I tried to do that! I scraped more fences and ran over more curbs!"

We all know, it takes practice to do something well—from baking a lemon meringue pie to playing a decent round of golf or teaching third grade. We also know mistakes are inevitable when trying to master any skill or art. If we can accept such failures while learning to bake a souffle or crochet an afghan, then why aren't we more accepting of the failures we make while learning to become a better person? Dare we even begin to see failure as a gift of the Spirit?

Maybe we can if we view failure not as an end in itself, but as a stage in a process. When we fail, then, instead of crying, "I've failed!" and throwing up our hands in defeat, we could say, "I've failed here. Now what can I learn from this?" or "Where do I go from here?"

Years ago I read an article entitled "The Theology of Failure." The title stuck with me, for I believe, as Christians, failure must be a part of our theology or our theology is lacking. After all, Christianity is rooted in the cross. And what is the cross but one humongous failure? Sometimes we forget that—maybe because we see too many pretty crosses—gold and silver ones, some with roses painted all over them. We forget that the cross was first and foremost an instrument of death and torture. Our wearing of a cross around our neck would be comparable to a French Revolutionary sporting a tiny guillotine, or a contemporary American a replica of the electric chair.

We also forget Christianity is rooted in failure because we know the *final* ending of Jesus' story. We know it did not end with that cross; it ended with that empty tomb. But Jesus did not know that for sure when he sweated blood in Gethsemane. And certainly his followers did not know it when they laid his mutilated body in the tomb. As far as they were concerned, it was over. All over. Jesus was a great guy, yes, but now he was dead. A total failure. End of story.

That is what the two disciples on the road to Emmaus think as they shuffle along, sharing their shock and disillusionment with each other (Luke 24:13–35). They share their disillusionment also with a certain stranger who happens along and joins them on their way. "We had hoped..." they say to him again and again. That stranger, of course, is Jesus. Gently and persistently, he opens the Scriptures to them with such force and clarity that their hearts begin to burn within them. Finally, in an instant, they recognize him in the breaking of the bread, and realize: death is but a stepping-stone to eternal life, failure, a bridge to everlasting glory!

Have any of my mistakes and failures been a gift of the Spirit?

✠ Jesus, help me to see my mistakes and failures as stepping-stones toward becoming a better person.

Faith

Belief is a wise wager.
—Blaise Pascal

I remember the first time my father let me ride the tractor. I was probably about five. My father crawled up onto the tractor first, leaned over, and with one effortless motion of his giant arm, swooped me up into the seat with him. Perched there in front of him, I felt very important—and a little afraid. The seat was higher than it looked from down below.

Next my father said, "Ready?" I nodded my head up and down real fast. "Good," he said. "Now you steer." Immediately I grabbed the steering wheel with both hands. He turned the key, the engine turned over, and the tractor shook beneath us. Over the roar of the motor, he said in my ear, "Now hang on," and he gently released the clutch. The tractor lurched forward. Instinctively I tightened my hands around the steering wheel. The tractor moved slowly at first, and then my father gave it more gas and we went a little faster, bouncing up and down together over the fields.

Too bad I don't have a picture of my father and me on the tractor that first time. If I did, I know what I would see. There am I, back arched, arms stiff, hands clenching the steering wheel. On my face is a look of grim determination. After all, I am steering this tractor! I am making it go straight! I am preventing it from going into the ditch! Or at least I think I am. The photo would also show my father smiling, his one hand unobtrusively on the steering wheel, his other wrapped around my waist, holding me gently but firmly in place. He is smiling, because he knows the truth. *He* is in control of that tractor. And *he* will see that no harm comes to me.

For me, riding the tractor with my father is a very good image of faith. Faith means being up high and moving forward. It means being eager, but maybe a little afraid too. It means keeping your hands on the steering wheel and doing your part. But most importantly, faith means knowing whose hands are on the wheel with yours. It means knowing who is sitting with you and whose arms are cradling you. It means knowing that no real harm can come to you. No matter what.

The problem is, sometimes we use the wrong synonyms for faith; for example, the word "creed." Kathleen Norris, in *Amazing Grace,* says it is a mistake to reduce faith to dogmas. Faith is "not a list of 'things I believe,'" she writes, "but the continual process of learning (and relearning) what it means to love God, my neighbor, and myself." Faith, then, is not something I have, but rather it is someone I am becoming—a more loving person.

Sometimes we think faith means certainty. When we have doubts, then, we think we don't have faith. No, faith can co-exist with doubts and uncertainties. In fact, doubts can actually nourish faith. Or sometimes we can equate faith with strength. "If my faith were stronger, I wouldn't be crying like this!" No, faith doesn't turn us into stoics. It doesn't necessarily calm the butterflies in our stomach, remove the lump from our throat, or wipe away our tears. We can be curled up in a little ball, sobbing our heart out, and still be a person of faith (see the chapter on BEREAVEMENT).

Sometimes we say, "My faith needs to be stronger." And, like an athlete gearing up to run a marathon, we grit our teeth and do all kinds of spiritual contortions to make our faith stronger. The truth is, even weak faith is still faith. A friend gave me this quote: "Strong faith in a weak plank will get you wet. But weak faith in a strong plank will get you to the shore." Perhaps if we focused less on our faith and more on the "Plank" to which we're clinging, we would be better off.

For me, the best synonym for faith is trust. The word trust usually implies another person. That Person, of course, is God who is riding the tractor with us over the bumpy fields and steering us safely home.

What is my favorite image of faith? What helps me to trust in God?

✚ God, give me a sense of your presence so I may enjoy our ride together more!

Forgiveness

Forgiveness is having given up all hope of having a better past.
—Anne Lamott

One way to appreciate the gift of forgiveness is to see it incarnated in a real human being.

On January 7, 1985 in Beirut, Lebanon, Father Lawrence Jenco, a program director for Catholic Relief Services, was kidnapped by Shiite Muslims. He was held hostage for 564 days. In his book, *Bound to Forgive,* Jenco describes his time in captivity—the terror, the torture, the isolation. While reading it, one marvels how Jenco could survive such an ordeal. But one marvels even more at Jenco's ability to forgive his captors for all they had done to him.

In an interview shortly after the book came out (*U.S. Catholic,* March 1996), a reporter asked Jenco how long it took him to start forgiving his captors. Jenco replied, "From day one." He went on to explain, "When you read the Scriptures, God's words of forgiveness appear throughout...If you don't forgive, you end up with a tremendous amount of hate and resentment." In fact, when he thought he was going to die in captivity, Jenco wanted to do so with the words of Jesus on his lips, "Father, forgive them for they know not what they do."

Although Jenco forgave his captors, he did not forget what they had done to him. "People say, 'Oh, forgive and forget' as if it's a mandate from God," he said. "But it doesn't work that way. I have all kinds of memories, and when I recall, I heal." When asked if he would tell others they ought to forgive, Jenco replied, "You must ask God for that gift. We are constantly going to God to ask for forgiveness, so why don't we ask God for the generosity to forgive as God forgives?"

Not many of us will end up being hostages like Jenco. Yet we can learn much about forgiveness from his experience. "The essence of my faith commitment is love," said the priest. "And the core of that is forgiveness." When Jenco shared his experience with people, some of them wept. Jenco believed they were not really crying for him, but rather because Jenco had touched their own pain and suffering, and even sometimes their own lack of forgiveness. He told how a woman came up to him after his talk once and cried, "Father, my sister and I go to Mass every morning. We haven't spoke in forty years. She sits on one side of the church, I sit on the other just in case at the kiss of peace I might have to extend peace to her." Father Jenco added, "What good is going to Mass every morning when this is going on?"

Like Jenco, we too are called to forgive those who do us wrong. This can be a tremendous challenge for us. I was reminded of this every time I taught forgiveness to high school students. Although many would accept this teaching in theory, they would often balk at its application in concrete situations. I remember one freshman boy in particular who, on a test, wrote a magnificent essay on forgiveness. But at the end he added this note to me: "This is what you taught us, Sister. But I still don't believe it. If someone harms me or a friend, I plan to get even with them! It's only fair!"

It's only fair. The boy was right. Forgiveness is *not* fair. But Jesus does not call us to fairness. He calls us to love. He calls us to become more like God. Joan Puls, OSF, describes forgiveness in these words: "Forgiveness is an act by which we enter into the realm of divine action. We behave as sons and daughters of a merciful God in whose image we are fashioned."

And so, we forgive. Everyone. We forgive the man who cuts in front of us in traffic as well as the spouse who embarrasses us at the party. We forgive our church, our nation, our human race. And, yes, we even forgive ourselves. And the reason we forgive is simple. As Father Jenco said, forgiveness is "the cost of being a follower of Jesus. You have to make Jesus' message a part of your life. You have to be the sacrament to the world of Jesus' love."

Am I a forgiving person? Have I ever experienced the forgiveness of another?

✠ Jesus, Forgiving One, help me to be the sacrament of your forgiveness in my own little part of the world.

Fortitude

With God, nothing, not even a headache, is lost.
—Blessed Lydwina of Scheidam

Several years ago the French painter André Girard was attending the opening of a chapel he had decorated. A woman approached him and said, "Mr. Girard, I do not like your crucifixion. It is so unpleasant." "Madame," Girard replied, "it was an unpleasant occasion."

As Christians, we are sometimes uncomfortable with unpleasantness. We prefer, for example, to dwell on the nice things Jesus said: "You are worth more than many sparrows" (Matthew 10:31); "Do not be afraid, little flock" (Luke 12:32); "Peace be with you" (John 20:19). We sometimes gloss over the other things Jesus said that aren't quite so pleasant: "Whoever wishes to come after me must deny himself, take up his cross, and follow me" (Matthew 16:24); "Behold I am sending you like sheep in the midst of wolves" (Matthew 10:16); and "I have come to set a man against his father, a daughter against her mother" (Matthew 10:35).

Unpleasantness, of course, is a fact of life. We find it even in Jesus' "nicest" parables. Before the Good Samaritan came along and ministered so lovingly to the man lying on the side of the road, a group of hoodlums had first robbed the man, beaten him to a pulp, and left him for dead. Before the prodigal son was welcomed back into his father's outstretched arms, he had insulted his father, squandered a fortune on loose living, and wallowed in the mud with pigs. And although poor, sore-covered Lazarus was eventually relieved of his misery and given an eternal reward, the rich man who had been blind to Lazarus' suffering, was punished for his lack of compassion.

Sometimes we Christians even downplay the crucifixion. After Vatican II, there was a movement to remove Jesus' body altogether from the cross or, at least, to replace the twisted, dead corpus with a triumphantly risen one. Yes, Jesus is risen. Yes, he will never die again. Yes, our faith is anchored in the reality of that empty tomb. But the fact remains: Jesus was raised only after he had passed through the extreme unpleasantness of the crucifixion. And we will be raised with Jesus only after we have passed through considerable unpleasantness of our own. Walter Burghardt, SJ, reminds us of the importance of the cross to our faith when he says: "a spirituality not intimately nailed to Calvary is a Christian mirage."

The gift of the Holy Spirit that keeps our spirituality nailed to Calvary is called fortitude. It is the gift that enables us to endure and/or work through pain and suffering. In his book, *For You Departed*, South African writer Alan Paton tells the poignant story of the death of his wife, a death characterized by prolonged suffering. Throughout the book, Paton addresses his deceased wife directly. At one point he writes, "Where did your courage come from? It was your religion, of course, that strange Christianity of yours that took seriously the story of the cross, that understood with perfect clarity that one might have to suffer for doing what was right, that rejected absolutely that kind of crossless geniality that calls itself Christianity."

What crosses does the gift of fortitude help us to endure? Here are just a few: difficulties with relationships, ill health, fears of all kinds, ambiguity, misunderstandings, failure, personal shortcomings, a sense of powerlessness, addictive behaviors, selfishness, loneliness, discouragement, and of course death. Our faith does not remove these sufferings. It helps us through them. Writer Mike Yaconelli says it well: "Faith is not the way around pain, it is the way through pain. Faith doesn't get rid of the opposition, it invites it over for dinner...Faith doesn't give you the solution, it forces you to find it."

Our model of fortitude, of course, is Jesus on the cross. But when we reflect on the crucifixion, it is important to look beneath the sufferings Jesus endured and see the love that made his endurance possible. As Anthony Padovano says, "Christ does not suffer because suffering is in itself a value, but because love without restraint requires suffering. It is not a love for suffering which Christ reveals, but a love which prevails in suffering."

The love that prevails in suffering is another name for fortitude.

What are some of the crosses I am bearing right now? How is my faith helping me to endure and/or work through these sufferings?

✝ Spirit, give me the gift of fortitude that my love may prevail in everything I do or endure.

Gentleness

You can no more win a war than you can win an earthquake.
—Jeannette Rankin

We live in a world of violence. Every day our news media run stories of women being murdered by their boyfriends, teenagers overdosing on drugs, bombs exploding in marketplaces, young girls being raped on their way to school, store clerks being shot in robberies, criminals being executed by the state, war planes bombing rebel forces. Then there's the violence that goes largely unreported, but is just as real: spouses screaming profanities at each other, teachers humiliating students in front of others, women opting for abortions, neighbors spreading gossip about neighbors, parents swatting kids on the head, kids punching other kids on the playground, women bashing men and men bashing women.

And into this mess steps Jesus who says, "Learn of me, for I am gentle and humble of heart" (Matthew 11:29). And we want to say, "Are you kidding? Gentle? Humble? In this day and age?" And Jesus is likely to reply, "Yes, in this day and age. More than ever."

What exactly is the gift of gentleness? Perhaps we can say that gentleness is a welcoming disposition toward life—all of life. That includes God (of course), others, myself and the whole of creation. Although we do not hear much about gentleness these days, it certainly is mentioned a lot in Scripture—especially in the New Testament. Jesus counseled gentleness by both word and action. One of his Beatitudes was about gentleness, "Blessed are the meek" (Matthew 5:5). Meekness is another word for gentleness. Jesus told his followers to turn the other cheek when they were struck rather than retaliate (Luke 6:29). When his apostles wanted to call down fire on the Samaritan village that refused to receive him, Jesus "rebuked them" for even considering such a violent thing (Luke 9:51–55). And when his enemies came to arrest him in the garden (John 18), and Peter clumsily tried to defend him by chopping off the ear of the high priest's slave, Jesus ordered, "Put your sword back into its sheath—for Pete's sake!" (I added that last part. It seemed to fit.) Jesus was gentle all the way to his unjust execution on the cross, thus giving us an incredible ideal to strive for: to be gentle and nonviolent even amid persecution.

How do we even begin to measure up to such an ideal of gentleness? We begin by acknowledging that we have the capacity to be very "ungentle," that is, to hurt, maim, or even kill. All of us do. No exceptions. I was reminded of this when, years ago, I was reading the newspaper one day beside an elderly nun with a cane. She had just read a dreadful article about a 1-year-old baby girl who had been severely beaten by her mother's boyfriend. The sister became furious. As she got up to leave, she banged her cane onto the floor several times and yelled, "That man should be shot! He should be shot!" I thought, if that man had suddenly appeared in the room, that nun would have whacked him to death with her cane! The point is, we are all capable of doing violence—even an elderly nun. Even me. Admitting that is the first step toward becoming more gentle.

We can also become more gentle by becoming more aware of the little ways we do violent things. Thomas Merton once said that when he undertook to become nonviolent, he started by closing doors softly. Perhaps we can start there too. Then we can move on to other things like: walking more slowly, speaking more respectfully to people—especially those who share the same house with us, using gender inclusive language, letting someone else go ahead of us in the checkout line, driving less frantically, eating foods that are healthy for us, visiting an elderly friend, volunteering at a shelter for abused women, getting more involved in promoting justice, praying for peace in our hearts and in the world.

Gentleness is not weakness. It is strength. It is not cowardliness. It is courage. But it is also somewhat unnatural. The natural response to life's pricks or stabs is to lash out in violence. As disciples of Jesus, however, we embrace another way, the way of gentleness. It is a gentleness rooted in the trust of a God who loves us more than we can begin to imagine.

How gentle am I toward others and myself? Have I ever turned the other cheek?

✚ Gentle Jesus, give me a gentle heart even amid persecution.

Guilt

Each snowflake in an avalanche pleads not guilty.
—Stanislaw Lee

There are two kinds of guilt. One is a gift of the Holy Spirit. The other is a trick of the Evil Spirit. Let's begin with the first one.

We live in an age that belittles guilt. Whenever we talk about guilt—whether it's Catholic guilt, Irish guilt, feminine guilt, or just plain guilty guilt—we usually do so in a pejorative way. Our culture tells us, "Guilt is bad." Or, worse yet, "You shouldn't feel guilty about anything." Even when we do some apparently bad things—spit at people, cheat on a test, steal a car, or even kill someone—we don't have to feel guilty. We can always blame something or someone else for our bad behavior: "The devil made me do it...My rotten childhood made me do it...My genes made me do it...Society made me do it." In a nation of victims, guilt is a rare commodity.

And that's too bad. Because guilt, properly understood, is a gift of the Spirit. It is one of the ways the Spirit directs our decision making. Guilt can encourage us to do the right thing, to make choices that are life-giving, and to feel sorry when our choices don't measure up to our dignity as children of God. Guilt, in this healthy sense, is largely an acceptance of responsibility for wrongdoing. When we scream at our spouse because of something that happened at work, for example, we should feel guilty. When we never have time for our loved ones, we should feel guilty. When we cling selfishly to our time and resources, we should feel guilty. When 1.5 billion people in this world are impoverished beyond any shred of human dignity, we should feel guilty.

A while back, Christine Gudorf wrote a fine article with an intriguing title: "Don't Cancel that Guilt Trip" (*U.S. Catholic,* Jan. 1995). In it she discusses the benefits of this healthy form of guilt. She writes, "In a well-formed conscience, guilt feelings are the warning bells that call us to repentance and conversion." Guilt, then, is good because it is often the first step toward seeking God's forgiveness. It is also the first step toward changing our life for the better. When the prodigal son returns to his father, he doesn't say, "The devil made me do it, Dad." No, he humbly acknowledges, "I have sinned." And his father responds with a quick, "Then let the party begin!"

But guilt, like many other gifts of the Spirit, can be manipulated by the Evil Spirit. In other words, guilt can be twisted into a form that is spiritually unhealthy or even lethal. This happens when, instead of urging us to run into the arms of our forgiving God, guilt paralyzes us. It makes us focus on our sins and forget about repentance or conversion. (In some ways, that's easier!) Guilt is bad if we wallow in it. This happens when we constantly stand before God (or curl up in the fetal position before God), beat our breasts, and cry out how wretched we are. We may be wretched—more or less—but there is nothing life-giving about wallowing in wretchedness. As Father Joseph Creedon says so well: "All of us are sinners: big deal. All of us are forgiven by God: now *that* is a big deal."

It is fascinating to note, when reading the lives of the saints, how many of them saw themselves as grave sinners. They seemed very comfortable with acknowledging their guilt and sin not only before God, but before the whole world. But notice, they didn't stop with their sin. They always went on to speak of God's great love. A saint in point is St. Paul. Paul saw himself as a great sinner. He had good reason, too. After all, didn't he participate in rounding up Christians for food for hungry lions? Didn't he participate in the stoning of St. Stephen? Talk about guilt! But Paul never described himself as a sinner without, at the same time, referring to God's grace which not only forgave him, but enabled him to be a useful instrument in the furthering of God's Kingdom. Without minimizing his sins, Paul refused to be paralyzed by them. As such, he is a fine example of what a healthy sense of guilt can do for all of us.

Have I ever experienced guilt as the first step toward repentance and conversion? Have I ever wallowed in guilt?

✠ God, I have sinned. May my sense of guilt lead me to make life-giving choices.

Healing

*You are the salve that purifies our souls; you are
the ointment that heals our wounds.*
—Hildegard of Bingen

The four evangelists are unanimous on this point: Jesus was a healer. In Mark's gospel, for instance, Jesus bursts onto the public scene amid a flurry of healing activity. In rapid succession he cures a raving demoniac in the synagogue, the feverish mother-in-law of Peter, a leper with open sores, a paralytic who had been lowered through the roof, and a man with a withered hand. Mark indicates that these healings were but a few examples of the many miracles Jesus worked. The other three evangelists paint a similar picture of Jesus. In fact, Matthew places this summary at the beginning of Jesus' ministry: "He went around all of Galilee, teaching in their synagogues, proclaiming the gospel of the kingdom, and curing every disease and illness among the people" (Matthew 4:23).

The truth is, however, Jesus did not cure every disease and illness. In fact, if we read the gospels carefully, we will see that, despite all the cures he wrought, Jesus was something of a reluctant healer. In fact, Jesus seldom took the initiative in curing others. He didn't run up and down the hills of Galilee curing every sick person in sight. No, ordinarily the sick had to come to him and specifically ask for a cure. Only on rare occasions—for example, the cure of the son of the widow of Naim—did Jesus himself initiate the healing.

Why this reluctance to heal people? For one thing, Jesus knew there was something far more important than physical healings. Namely, faith. In fact, most of Jesus' cures were a direct response to someone's faith. Jesus emphasized this link between healing and faith on numerous occasions. He said to the woman with the hemorrhage, "Daughter, your faith has saved you" (Mark 5:34). After restoring sight to the blind Bartimaeus, Jesus told him, "Go your way; your faith has saved you" (Mark 10:52). Before raising Jairus' little girl from the dead, he said to him, "Do not be afraid; just have faith" (Mark 5:36).

Conversely, the lack of faith made healings downright impossible. Jesus was unable "to perform any mighty deed" in his own hometown of Nazareth, for example, because of the people's "lack of faith"—a lack that "amazed" even Jesus (Mark 6:1–6). A little later, the Pharisees demanded from him some sort of spectacular sign so they might be convinced of his authority. But Jesus staunchly refused: "He sighed from the depth of his spirit and said, 'Why does this generation seek a sign? Amen, I say to you, no sign will be given to this generation'" (Mark 8:12). As theologian Donald Senior, CP, has said, "Jesus never used miracles to bludgeon people into belief."

Ultimately, though, Jesus came among us to heal not bodies, but souls. After all, every person Jesus healed during his ministry eventually died. The point of the cures was not to extend earthly life forever. The point was to restore eternal life now—and the cures were but a sign of that restoration. Jesus, therefore, was far more interested in restoring spiritual sight than physical sight. He was more concerned with cleansing from sin than from leprosy. His basic call was not, "Be healed!" It was, "Repent!" The Cistercian monk Thomas Keating sees a connection between repentance and healing. In fact, he calls repentance "that fundamental call in the Gospel to begin the healing process."

This gift of the Holy Spirit reminds us that we are all ill no matter how healthy we may be physically. We all suffer from maladies of the soul. What are some of those spiritual maladies? We may be crippled by guilt, paralyzed by fear, blind to the truth, deaf to the cry of the poor. Or we may be imprisoned by addictive behaviors, bent over from despair, or living with a broken heart. The healing process begins when we repent, that is, turn to Jesus and hear him ask us, as he asked so many sick people in the Gospels, "What would you like me to do for you?"

And may we simply say to him, "Heal me...Heal me...Heal me." And may we do whatever Jesus tells us to do to begin the healing process.

What are some of my spiritual maladies? Do I really believe Jesus can heal me?

✝ Healing Jesus, make me whole!

Initiative

If you just sit around and wait, the only
thing that happens is you get older.
—Anonymous

When I was planning this book, I glanced over my list of tentative chapters and saw words such as gentleness, patience, piety, lowliness. I feared if people were to read only those titles, they could get the wrong impression and mistakenly conclude that the gifts of the Holy Spirit were essentially passive. If people actually read those chapters, of course, they will see that is not true. But still, I made the decision to include some gifts that were unmistakenly non-passive. This is one of those gifts: initiative.

Initiative means to start something, to take the first step. It means to not sit around on your fanny waiting for someone else to do something, but to get up off the couch and do it yourself. Jesus appreciated initiative. He seemed pleased, for example, that a few of the disciples (including Andrew) came to him on their own initiative (John 1:35–42), thus saving him the trouble of seeking them out. Jesus also seemed to enjoy the persevering initiative of the Canaanite woman who refused to take no for an answer, but kept bugging Jesus until she nearly drove the apostles crazy. They pleaded with him to give her her little miracle already, for crying out loud! (Matthew 15:21–28). And Jesus must have laughed when he saw the heights to which Zacchaeus' initiative carried him—to the top of that sycamore tree. Jesus rewarded Zak's initiative, too, by calling him down and dining in his house—much to the shock of the self-righteous and more passive onlookers (Luke 19:1–10).

Jesus not only appreciated initiative when he saw it, he encouraged it when he didn't see it. He once told his disciples to be simple as doves, yes, but clever as serpents. Cleverness presupposes a certain amount of initiative, don't you think? Besides, have you ever met a cobra that was a doormat? Jesus also told a parable about a steward with an incredible amount of initiative. Rather than wait around for his master to fire him because of some crooked things he had done, the steward cleverly arranged things to insure himself a warm welcome from others when he was thrown out into the street. Now that was initiative!

Jesus encouraged initiative in his disciples mainly by calling them to action. He didn't say, "Now you guys just sit around here and wait until the people come to you." No, he sent them out—all seventy-two of them—to go where the people were to preach the good news—proactively. When Jesus spoke about forgiveness, he didn't say, "Now you just wait here until the other guy or gal comes to you." No, he told them—in no uncertain terms—that they were to take the initiative in forgiving others. In fact, so important was it to take the first step in forgiving that nothing was to interfere with this initiative—not even the worship of God.

But the biggest news that Jesus proclaimed about initiative though was this: God is the Great Initiator. God is the great Starter-of-Everything. After all, it was God who literally began everything with the first "Let there be light!" But God not only initiated creation, God also initiated salvation. It was God who heard the Israelites moaning and groaning in slavery in Egypt and decided it was time to set up an appointment with Moses at a local burning bush. It was God who heard the human race moaning and groaning in the slavery of sin and decided it was time to tell Gabe to dust off his wings and hightail it down to Nazareth. And it was God who, represented by the father in the parable of the Prodigal Son, ran out to greet his ingrate of a son and smother him with kisses and rings, and threw a big bash for him.

The gift of initiative reminds us that, as Christians, we are called to action. We are called to start things. We are called not merely to respond to life's events, but to play an active role in determining their course. By doing so, we will become more and more like our God, the Initiator of All.

Have I taken any initiative lately to spread the Good News? Do I play an active role in determining the course of my life?

✠ Initiating Spirit, help me to start something good today!

Instinct

A good person is not one who does the right thing, but one who is in the habit of doing the right thing.
—Abraham Heschel

When we hear the word "instinct" many of us immediately think, "Instinct is something animals have to insure their survival and propagation." When we see a beagle scooting across a field with his nose to the ground (looking like a little vacuum cleaner!), that's instinct. When we see a pair of geese mating on a pond, amid the flutter of wings and the splashing of water, that's instinct too.

But humans also have instincts. I learned in biology class years ago that infants are born with two instincts: to suck and to cry. Infants begin to suck while they are still in the womb, gearing up their little mouths for their first taste of milk! Then there is the other instinct: crying. Crying is the instinct a baby has to communicate that something is wrong and, thus, better assure its survival. Experienced mothers can even identify what type of cry it is. "WAHHH! I want my diaper changed!" is different from "WAHHH! I'm hungry!" or "WAHHH! I have gas!"

Because we tend to identify instinct with animals, we often equate it with our so-called "animal nature." Sex is an instinct, we say. So is the drive to get ahead, to accumulate wealth, to bully others. The story of the "fall" in Genesis reinforces our conception that instinct is bad. Because of the sin of our first parents, all of us are essentially corrupt, some say. But the doctrine of the total corruption of humankind is hard to reconcile with experience. When I was sixteen years old, for instance, I met a boy my age who, two years earlier, had rushed into a burning house to rescue two small boys who had been playing with matches. Considerable attention was given to his act of heroism, including the awarding of a medal. But the boy confided to me that he felt uncomfortable with all the fuss. "At the time, I never even thought of the danger to myself," he said. "I just thought of getting those kids out!" Wasn't that instinct—in a good sense?

54

We are made in the image and likeness of God. Then surely that means some of our instincts are Godlike. *Some* are. The trick, of course, is being able to identify those instincts that are Godlike and those that are not. Jesus gave us a litmus test to discern the difference. His words about distinguishing between true and false prophets can also help us to distinguish between good and bad instincts: "By their fruits you will know them" (Matthew 7:16). We can ask ourselves: If I follow this instinct, what will it do to me, my relationships, my goals, my level of happiness? Does following this instinct bring peace, self-esteem, a sense of harmony, joy?

The better I get as a writer, the more I can trust my instincts with regard to writing. This means I do not have to agonize over every word choice, every structural option—as I had to do when I first began writing. No, after years of writing experience, I can allow my instinct to direct me in both word choice and structural option. Something similar happens with regard to our spiritual lives. The better we get as Christians, the more we can trust our instincts. This means we do not have to agonize over every choice we make.

As a writer, though, I do not rely solely on my instincts. I submit my writing to friends and editors who read what I write and periodically offer me feedback. Sometimes they say, "This is great, Melannie! Keep it up!" And other times, "This is basically good, but can I make a few suggestions?" As Christians, we need such friends and "editors of the spiritual life" (like a good spiritual director) to give us feedback on the choices we are making, the instincts we are following. For, the fact remains, our instincts, no matter how noble they seem or how well they have served us in the past, could still lead us astray.

But the truth is, good instincts have their origin in God. Maybe good instincts are simply another name for Grace.

What are some of my good instincts? Who are some of the "editors of my spiritual life"?

✚ Gracious God, help me to follow those instincts of mine that have their origin in you!

Intimacy

True knowledge leads to love.
—William Wordsworth

If you are looking for the chapter on the gift of knowledge, this is it. Why I am calling it "intimacy" will become clear in a minute. But first, let's look at that word "knowledge."

When we hear the word "knowledge," we usually think of things that we grasp with our intellect, that is, facts and ideas. We know, for example, that 2 + 2 = 4, the earth revolves around the sun, and Lake Michigan is located west of Michigan. But in the Bible, the word "know" means something more than that. It means to experience something directly. If I "know" Lake Michigan in the biblical sense, that does not simply mean I can point to it on a map; it means I have *experienced* Lake Michigan, that is, I have seen it, sailed it, fished in it, swum in it, and even drunk it. Similarly, if I know another person in the biblical sense, that does not mean I am merely acquainted with them. It means I know them personally—through and through. In fact, sometimes in the Bible, the word "know" means to have sexual intercourse. We read in Genesis, for example, that Adam "knew" Eve and she conceived a son (Genesis 4:1). The deepest kind of knowledge in scriptural terms, therefore, is intimacy.

What exactly is intimacy? First of all, it is not the same as having sex. Two people can have a deep, intimate relationship without ever engaging in sex. Conversely, two people can have sex and not have an intimate relationship. Second, intimacy involves a relationship between *two persons*. Both words are important. *Two:* I cannot be intimate by myself. *Persons:* Nor can I truly be intimate with anything except another person. Yes, I can have an affectionate relationship with my dog or parakeet or even my car, but intimacy presupposes a deeper kind of sharing that can exist only between two persons.

Third, intimacy involves a mutual sharing between those persons. If only one person shares, that is not intimacy. Intimacy presupposes that I allow myself to be known by the other, and I allow the other person to make himself or herself known to me. It is a relationship of mutual respect in which both parties can be who they are. And finally, intimacy takes time. Strictly speaking, we cannot have an intimate relationship with someone we have known for only five minutes or even five days. The depth of sharing involved in intimacy presupposes a significant length of association.

With regard to intimacy, the "good news" of the Bible is this: God desires intimacy with us. God called Abraham not only to a new homeland, but also to a deep, personal relationship with him—a relationship characterized by honesty, mutual give-and-take, and trust. Scripture is replete with other individuals who were on intimate terms with God—Jacob, Moses, Joseph, Gideon, Judith, Ruth, David, Joseph, Mary. Their lives demonstrated that God wishes to know us and to be known by us.

The clearest evidence of God's desire for intimacy with us, however, is the person of Jesus. In fact, we can say that Jesus' coming into our world proves just how much God wants to know us and be known by us. Jesus was on intimate terms with God, going so far as to call God "Abba." He was on intimate terms with his disciples, saying to them at the Last Supper, "I call you friends" (John 15:15). He encouraged intimacy among his followers, calling them to mutual love and forgiveness, intimacy's two greatest tools.

Today we might want to ask ourselves, with whom do I have an intimate relationship? How do I nurture intimacy with others? Have I ever experienced God's desire to be intimate with me? How do I share myself with God and allow God to share him/herself with me? Today we might want to pray Psalm 139, too, one of the most beautiful expressions of our intimate relationship with God: "God, you know me...you know when I sit and when I stand...you understand my thoughts from afar...Probe me, God, and know my heart."

In what ways has intimacy been a gift for me personally? What have been some of the challenges of intimacy?

✠ God, I thank you for the gift of intimacy! Let me experience today your desire to know me and to be known by me.

Kindness

When I was young, I admired clever people.
Now that I am old, I admire kind people.
—Abraham Heschel

One day I came across this sentence: "Most people are kind, polite, and sweet-minded—until you try to get into their pew!" I like that, for it acknowledges just how hard it is to be kind—even in church. Why is kindness so difficult? For one thing, kindness is so darn close, so near at hand. It demands that I act in a selfless way to these human beings right in front of me or next to me: this coworker who cracks her gum all day, this elderly woman who talks incessantly, this teenage boy who is such a smart aleck, this next door neighbor who plays his music too loud.

Love, in contrast, can be more distant. Since Jesus calls us to love everybody, we can say, "I love the people in Sri Lanka," and probably mean it. But ordinarily, we cannot say we are kind to the people in Sri Lanka unless we are in Sri Lanka. No, it is far easier to love everybody who lives far away than it is to be kind to one single human being who lives next door.

Kindness is difficult also because it is so concrete. It almost always makes some specific, personal demand upon us. Kindness says, "Help carry those groceries—now! Offer to change that tire—now! Run to the store for milk—now!" Kindness is usually obvious, too. There's almost no mistaking kindness when you see it—or mistaking its absence when you do not. Love, on the other hand, does not always have to be that concrete or obvious. We can say we love our children, for example, even when we are disciplining them—and we are loving them! Love can be faked more easily than kindness, too. But faked kindness is easy to spot. It even has a name: obsequiousness.

Kindness is difficult for yet another reason. In his article entitled "Kindness" (*America*, Feb. 14, 1998), Father William O'Malley, SJ, says that kindness goes beyond the Golden Rule. He writes, "'Do unto others as you would have others do unto you,' is not the touchstone of any one religion; it is a matter of human survival....But kindness takes one step further, beyond morality, into unreflective loving."

Unreflective loving. That is a good definition of kindness. But how do we learn to be kind? How do we come to love unreflectively? We probably begin by seeing the kindness of others. When I was growing up on our small farm in Ohio, for example, I was being instructed in the ways of kindness without even knowing it. My mother used to bake quite regularly. Two of her specialties were apple pies and rye bread. On many occasions I can remember her saying, "Take the Stevensons this loaf of bread," or "Take this apple pie to Shinky" (the hired hand who lived on the farm next door). When road workers were fixing our road under the hot summer sun, my mother sent us kids out with a pitcher of water or lemonade for them. Similarly, my father, who always had a big garden, was forever giving things away—beans, tomatoes, strawberries, corn. The example of my parents' many acts of kindness, of unreflective loving, made a lasting impression on me.

Jesus calls us to love everybody. He also calls us to be kind to the specific individuals we meet each day. It is sometimes particularly challenging to be kind to the people we live with. That is because we see them so often, we tend to take them for granted—like the tile on the kitchen floor or the picture on the living room wall. Sometimes we can treat them like floor tile or a wall hanging, too. It is easy to drift into the habit of speaking curtly to the ones we live with, ignoring them, or being downright rude to them. Remember, Kindness, like her big sister Charity, always begins at home.

In his famous "Hymn to Charity" (1 Corinthians 13:1–13), St. Paul wisely says that love, if it is genuine, is kind. What does this mean on a practical level? It means letting someone into our pew with a smile— even if they are late!

How did I first learn about kindness? How kind am I now?

✙ Loving God, teach me to be kind.

Leadership

"If I, therefore, the master and teacher, have washed your feet,
you ought to wash one another's feet."
—Jesus

One of the great leaders of the church in our day was Cardinal Joseph Bernardin of Chicago. As Bernardin lay in a hospital recuperating from cancer surgery, his friend Eugene Kennedy delivered an eloquent testimony to him at the annual meeting of the U.S. bishops. What Kennedy said about Bernardin can be applied to any good leader: he "has never been afraid of the dark and, in his company, neither are we." People like Cardinal Bernardin teach us a lot about leadership. In this chapter, I would like to share eight lessons I have learned about the gift of leadership from people such as Bernardin.

1. Leadership is the capacity to influence others for the better. Good leadership is always directed toward liberation.

2. There are various forms of leadership—charismatic, administrative, executive, to name a few. Each type has both positive and negative aspects. The type that is best for a particular group will vary according to time, place, and circumstances.

3. Exercising leadership is not the same as exercising authority. As Richard McCormick, SJ, from Notre Dame has said, "One can command all day without being a leader for a minute."

4. We can be a leader without wearing a badge, carrying a crosier, banging a gavel, or sitting behind a big desk. Parents and teachers, for example, are leaders. In fact, all Christians, by virtue of their baptism, are called to some form of leadership.

5. Jesus had some revolutionary ideas about leadership. One day, an argument broke out among his apostles as to which of them was the greatest. This happened toward the end of Jesus' life. We can only begin to imagine what Jesus must have felt when he heard his closest followers bickering over rank. He probably wanted to scream, "Haven't you guys heard anything I've said?" But instead he said to them, "The kings

of the Gentiles lord it over them, and those in authority over them are addressed as 'Benefactors'; but among you it shall not be so. Rather, let the greatest among you be as the youngest, and the leader as the servant" (Luke 22:25–26).

6. At the Last Supper, Jesus gave his apostles (and us!) a memorable picture of the type of leadership he was calling for. Wrapping a towel around his waist and kneeling down, he began to wash the feet of his disciples. Leadership for Jesus, then, was never about privilege; it was always about service.

7. The poet William Butler Yeats wrote, "The real leader serves truth, not people." In other words, good leaders resist the temptation to merely please people. When a Howard University president was asked to name the fundamental quality of leadership, he replied, "The capacity to inflict pain." That was his blunt way of saying that leadership requires the courage to speak the truth (to serve Truth) no matter how unpopular it might be.

8. Good leaders do not make tensions go away. James Bacik, a theologian and diocesan priest, says that what we need is a "dialectical spirituality," that is, one that understands the tensions of our age and allows them to bring forth good fruit. Some of those dialectical tensions include the following: the individual and community, spirituality and human development, the traditional and the new, the Gospel and culture, life and death, the eternal and the ever changing. Good leaders, like Jesus, befriend paradox.

In her book, *The Thread of Blue Denim,* Patricia Leimbach describes seeing a flock of migrating geese one fall afternoon. The sight evokes in her a reflection on leadership. She asks herself, "How would I choose a head goose if I were a goose and obliged to choose?" She answers, "I should certainly want to follow the wisest goose, the one with a sense of goose history...I should want a compassionate goose...I would want a leader who saw that we didn't eat so richly and so long that we could no longer fly." Leimbach then concludes with these words: "The most important question to consider in choosing a head goose? Is he headed in the right direction?"

Who for me has been a model of servant leadership? What are some of the ways I exercise leadership in my life?

✚ Jesus, help me to believe in leadership as compassionate service.

Learning

Each step is the place to learn.
—Sue Bender

When I think of the gift of learning, I think of my father. Dad never had the opportunity to go to college. He had the bad luck of graduating from high school in 1932—right in the middle of the Depression. As the oldest of six children, he dutifully got a job in an auto parts store to help support his family. But Dad was a learner *par excellence*. As a child, I seldom saw my father without a book, newspaper, or magazine in his hand. When we went to my grandparents on Thanksgiving, for example, while we kids ran off to the show in the afternoon and the other adults sat in the basement playing cards, my dad would sit contentedly in a living room chair reading some huge tome on electronics or the Civil War.

A tool and die maker by profession, Dad simultaneously ran his own goose farm and hatchery, learning by experience to make it a productive operation. He was good at fixing any kind of motor, too. If he was not under our car or tractor, he was tinkering with the neighbor's broken lawn mower until he got it to work again. Dad always did his own plumbing and electrical work, too. He also cultivated a huge garden where he grew everything from corn to kiwi. In addition, he planted an orchard and a vineyard and taught himself to make good wine and beer. In short, Dad was a learner. At age eighty-four, he still is!

When I reflected on the gift of learning, I came up with these observations. Learners are humble. That is so because they know they don't know everything. Once I lived with a sister everyone was having a hard time with. Another sister said to me, "The problem with her is she thinks she knows everything." I had to agree. Learners are easier to live with than non-learners. And they have more friends.

Learners also have more fun. That is because they are curious. When they do not know something, they do not say, "I don't know" and go back to lying on the couch. No, they say, "I don't know, but I'd like to find out," and they reach for an encyclopedia, click on the Internet, or run to the phone and call a friend who might know. Learners are seldom bored because they are always learning something new. Learners are seldom boring, either. They are *interesting* people because they are *interested* people—in everything from the stock market to the nightlife of the ring-tailed lemur of Madagascar.

Genuine learners can learn under any circumstances. They never wait for ideal conditions. If they are caught in a traffic jam, or their flight was canceled, or they are about to undergo toe surgery, they are learning something. All experiences—positive, negative, or somewhere in between—can teach them something new about themselves and about life. Learners tend to be flexible. They have to be, for every time they learn something new, they are changed by it. It is as if every new piece of information or insight or experience causes a new groove or wrinkle in their brain (or heart!).

Learners know the most effective way to learn something is through experience. They know there is a big difference between being told the flame is hot and actually putting your hand into the flame. At the same time, learners are very good at learning from the experience of others. They tend to be good listeners, good observers, and good readers. Still, in the final analysis, most learners would subscribe to the proverb that says, "When the book and bird disagree, believe the bird!"

Jesus liked learners. We learn this from the gospels. His favorite kind of people were individuals who were humble, curious, flexible, interesting, and open to change. In other words, learners. Conversely, Jesus had a hard time with individuals who thought they knew it all and refused to learn. For example, the Pharisees. One of Jesus' favorite words was "learn." He frequently invited his listeners to learn from his teachings and parables. And his main invitation was simply this: "Learn from me" (Matthew 11:29).

In conclusion, I have learned over the years that learning is a lot like yearning. Not only do the two words look and sound alike, they both eventually lead to the same end: Truth, which (after all) is but another name for God.

To what extent am I a learner? What have I learned recently from my own experience or the experience of others?

✚ God of Truth, may all my learning and yearning lead me to you today.

Levity

Those who believe in Christ will laugh unhesitatingly in everlasting glory.
—St. Pionius

Marc Gellman is a rabbi on Long Island. Tom Hartman is a priest also on Long Island. Several years ago they were both invited by a local cable TV station in New York to discuss the similarities between Passover and Easter. Says Hartman, "Right away, we hit it off. It was magic." Gellman agrees and adds, "Both Tom and I realized religion had not been covered well, or at all, by the media." The two men decided to do something about that. They offered to be "the religion guys" for a major TV network. Within a short time, they were appearing regularly on both TV and radio, discussing everything from prayer to suffering, from morals to death. They also wrote several books together including *Where Does God Live?* and *How Do You Spell God?*

But it is not just the fact that a rabbi and a priest are discussing religion together that is noteworthy. It is how they are discussing religion together—with wit and humor. Gellman explains, "One reason religion is not being listened to is that it takes itself so seriously. It's sometimes presented in such a humorless, accusatory, and guilt-provoking way that people's reaction is, 'I don't want any more of this.' It's sort of like castor oil."

Both men are convinced that God wants us to laugh. When asked what the best proof is that God has a sense of humor, Gellman replies, "The platypus. A god who could make an animal like that is definitely funny." Hartman adds, "And look around at the way God made people. You gotta laugh. People are very funny."

Father Hartman and Rabbi Gellman are doing everyone a big service by introducing levity into their discussions of religion. For religion and levity should go together. In fact, levity is one of the gifts of the Holy Spirit. Elton Trueblood, a Protestant minister, would agree. He warned, "Never trust a theologian who doesn't have a sense of humor." Similarly, Friedrich Nietzsche, a nineteenth-century German philosopher, once had a vision of Satan. Nietzsche described the devil as "the spirit of gravity."

In a world that constantly bombards us with bad news, levity is not easy to sustain. But levity is not blind to this bad news. On the contrary, it sees clearly the injustice and suffering around and within us. But levity believes that injustice and suffering, in light of God's promises, are never ultimate. Another way of saying that is this: levity sees further than gravity. It sees deeper. It sees more. Perhaps I can illustrate this with a little levity.

A father was watching what he thought was a family movie on TV with his eight-year-old son. Suddenly, one of the men in the movie asked a woman, "Why do you work as a lady of the night?" She replied, "So I will find $300 on my pillow in the morning." The little boy's eyes got real big. He turned to his father and said, "Boy, she must've had a big tooth!"

Why do we laugh at that story? Because we see more than the little boy sees. We see beyond the tooth fairy! Our perception of reality is much broader, hence, we laugh at the boy's remark, a remark based on his limited point of view. I like to think that when we finally enter heaven, we will begin to see things from God's perspective, the broadest and most far-reaching perspective of all. At that moment, we will begin to laugh—hysterically, wildly, uncontrollably—for at least the first thousand years!

Meanwhile, back here on earth, laughter does not always come so easily. In fact, levity actually demands self-denial. Theologian Jean Leclercq calls this the "asceticism of joy." He explains: Levity "involves the most difficult self-denial of all: you no longer take yourself too seriously. The days and nights no longer rotate around you, your heartaches and hiatal hernia, your problems, your frustrations." Instead, when we laugh, we see ourselves as we truly are, creatures of good and evil, strength and weakness, wisdom and folly.

Dr. John McBride, a psychotherapist, summed it up well when he said, "The ability to laugh at ourselves is the next greatest gift we have to love."

What is the current level of levity in my life? What helps me not to take myself so seriously?

✚ God of levity and laughter, help me to lighten up!

Liberation

Freedom is nothing else but the chance to be better.
—Albert Camus

As I stood in St. Wenceslaus Square in the heart of Prague a few years back, several images came to my mind. I recalled photographs of the uprising against the Communists in 1968. One picture in particular I remembered. It showed a young student waving a sign with my last name on it: Svoboda, that is, "freedom." Unfortunately, those cries for liberty in 1968 were answered with arrests, bullets, and tanks. The second image that came to my mind as I stood there were TV news clips of the revolution of 1989. This massive and largely peaceful uprising, unlike the one in 1968, proved successful, and the Czech people won their freedom (their "svoboda") from Communist oppression. Later as I listened to my relatives tell stories of what it was like to live under Communist rule for forty years, I thought, "Only those who have been enslaved can begin to appreciate liberation."

Liberation is one of the major themes in the Bible. In the Old Testament, the Greek word for liberation is *eleutheroo* which literally means "to be snatched from slavery." The Old Testament speaks of two great liberations: the freeing of Israel from the slavery of Egypt, and later from the slavery of Babylon. Both liberations were viewed as the direct result of the goodness and power of God.

When Jesus came onto the scene, he spoke of his mission in terms of liberation. Standing up in his hometown synagogue one Sabbath, he read a passage from the prophet Isaiah and identified himself with these words: "The Spirit of the Lord is upon me....He has sent me to proclaim liberty to captives" (Luke 4:18). Some of Jesus' listeners assumed he was speaking of political liberation, that is, the freeing of the Jews from Roman domination. It was a misunderstanding that plagued Jesus' ministry all the way to Calvary. Again and again Jesus tried to clarify that the type of liberation he was speaking of was not liberation from the Romans; it was liberation from sin. As the Biblical scholar Xavier Léon-

Dufour has said, "Sin is the true despot from whose yoke Jesus wrests us."

St. Paul, who knew a lot about liberation, claimed that Jesus also freed us from the law: "Sin is not to have any power over you, since you are not under the law but under grace" (Romans 6:14). This doesn't mean we ignore all law. Rather, it means we no longer look exclusively to exterior law for our principle of salvation. Instead, our new norm of conduct becomes docility to the Spirit poured out into our hearts (see the chapter on DISCERNMENT). Paul still speaks of the "law of Christ" on occasion, but this is "the new law" summed up best in the word "love."

When we think of freedom we think of words like independence and self-autonomy. We think, "No one is going to tell me what to do!" But Scripture paints a different picture. True liberty begins by knowing who we are: children of God. It means being free to hear the promptings of the Holy Spirit calling us to ever greater selflessness. It means becoming more and more like Jesus who became the servant of all.

What are the chief hindrances to this kind of liberty? One hindrance is forgetting our dignity as children of God. To deny personal responsibility for our actions by saying things like "The devil made me do it" implies that we belong more to the Evil Spirit than we do to God's Spirit. Another hindrance to achieving liberation is insensitivity to the needs of others. In the very name of freedom, we can live very selfish lives. Pope John Paul II reminds us, "The worst prison would be a closed heart." A third impediment to freedom is fear. Although we all claim we want to be free, the prospect of being really free can be downright terrifying. As George Bernard Shaw put it, "Liberty means responsibility. That is why most people dread it."

One final note: I called this gift of the Spirit not "freedom" but "liberation." I did this on purpose. Freedom sounds too much like a done deal to me, whereas liberation implies a process. And that's an important difference. For as it was once said, "Liberty is always unfinished business."

To what extent have I attained liberation? What gets in the way of my being free?

✚ God, thank you for making me your child! Jesus, thank you for freeing me from sin! Spirit, thank you for liberating me from selfishness!

Lowliness

Big doesn't necessarily mean better. Sunflowers aren't better than violets.
—Edna Ferber

John Ciardi has written a lovely poem entitled "The Size of Song." In it he makes an observation about the size of birds and their ability to sing. He says, "Some rule of birds kills off song/in any that begin to grow/ much larger than a fist or so." His observation seems true. Just compare the large crow with its strident "Caw! Caw!" and the tiny wren with its melodic "Tweet! Tweet! Tweet!" Or the giant ostrich who sings not at all with the tiny yellow canary who can't keep from warbling. In the world of birds, when it comes to song, small is beautiful.

In the world of Scripture, small is beautiful too. Take the Israelites. They were a small, insignificant nation, yet God said to them through Moses on Mount Sinai, "You shall be my special possession, dearer to me than all other people" (Exodus 19:5). On the eve of his great battle against the Midianites, Gideon was directed by God to make his army smaller not larger, that is, to trim it down from 22,000 to 300 (Judges 7). Later, God told the prophet Samuel to anoint David, the smallest and youngest of Jesse's sons, as king of Israel (1 Samuel 16:12–13). And when the prophet Elijah experienced God in the cave, God came not as a huge storm or powerful earthquake, but as "a still small voice, " or, as another translation puts it, "a tiny whispering sound" (1 Kings 19:12).

The New Testament also praises smallness in its many forms. Jesus is born of Mary, a young teenager from the small town of Nazareth who refers to herself in terms of lowliness: "Behold, I am the handmaiden of the Lord" (Luke 1:38). Mary gives birth to Jesus not in a spacious palace in the large city of Jerusalem, but in a cramped cave in the proverbial "little town of Bethlehem." Throughout his ministry, Jesus makes a big deal out of smallness. He chooses as his disciples mostly ordinary and insignificant individuals. Although he preaches his message to all, he directs it especially to the poor and the lowly. Later he compares the Kingdom of God to a tiny mustard seed. And Jesus tells his followers, if they wish to become his disciples, they must become as little children, they must strive to be the least. Finally, he says of himself, "I am meek and humble of heart" (Matthew 11:29).

Smallness. Lowliness. Meekness. Not exactly the watchwords of our day. On the contrary, ours is a world where "bigger is better," where we overuse the prefixes *mega, super,* and *ultra.* Ours is a culture that glorifies power and rewards audacity. Perhaps more than ever, then, we need this gift of the Spirit that enables us to respect smallness, celebrate lowliness, and befriend meekness.

This gift of lowliness helps us to appreciate smallness in all its forms: youth, inexperience, ordinariness, illness, poverty, powerlessness, incompleteness, inadequacy, pre-birth, old age. Today we might want to take a reality check of our attitude toward "least-ness." For example, how do I respond to children? Am I protective of their lives, attentive to their needs, concerned for their future? What about the elderly? Am I appreciative of their past accomplishments, patient with their infirmities, mindful of their well-being? How do I respond to the "lowly" I encounter in everyday life—the poor, the sick, the physically and mentally challenged, the ignorant, the imprisoned, the sinner?

How do I respond when I experience smallness and lowliness within myself? Am I content to be ordinary? Am I patient with my sins and failures? Do I acknowledge my shortcomings, my incompleteness? When I experience my powerlessness, what do I do? Throw up my hands in despair or reach out for the ever ready hand of God?

St. Paul not only accepted his lowliness, he boasted about it. To the Corinthians he wrote these magnificent words: "If I must boast, I will boast of the things that show my weakness" (2 Corinthians 11:30). Why? Because Paul heard and believed these words Jesus spoke to him: "My grace is sufficient for you, for power is made perfect in weakness" (2 Corinthians 12:9). May we, like Paul, be able to proclaim, "For when I am weak, then I am strong" (2 Corinthians 12:10).

What is my attitude toward smallness and lowliness? Do I really believe that God loves the lowly?

✝ God of the lowly, fill my weakness with your saving power.

Mercy

God is mercy within mercy within mercy.
—Thomas Merton

The spiritual and corporal works of mercy are a venerable tradition in the Church. In the chapter on COMPASSION, I said something about the corporal works of mercy. In this chapter, I would like to address the spiritual works of mercy. There are seven of them. Let's take a quick look at each one.

1. *Admonish the sinner.* This work of mercy is solidly based in Scripture. Jesus said, "If your brother (sister) sins, go and tell him (her) his (her) fault" (Matthew 18:15). St. Paul instructed the Colossians to "teach and admonish one another" (Colossians 3:16). This work of mercy is rooted in the belief that sin leads us away from God and others. It separates us from love and eventually ends in misery. Sometimes this work of mercy means telling people what they may not want to hear. That takes courage and tact. Most often, though, it means living our faith in such a way that others find it immensely attractive.

2. *Instruct the ignorant.* Good instruction helps people to see things in a new perspective. It has the power to change attitudes and transform behavior. Parents perform this work of mercy every time they teach their children how to be a better person. Catechists practice this work every time they step into a classroom. And all of us instruct the ignorant every time we share with others information that leads to further spiritual growth. This presupposes, of course, that we are open to the instruction of others too.

3. *Counsel the doubtful.* Doubt can assume many forms, but perhaps the most prevalent form in today's world is doubt about one's self-worth. We can help alleviate this doubt in others by addressing them respectfully, listening to them, complimenting them, doing small favors for them, offering encouraging words, asking them for help, thanking them, and spending time with them. The way we treat others can say to them, "You are good. You are worthwhile. There's no doubt about it!"

4. *Comfort the sorrowful.* Jesus comforted the sorrowful: the widow of Naim, the family of Jairus, and Mary and Martha when their brother died. Comforting the sorrowful is seldom easy. We tend to feel helpless, awkward, at a loss for words. It is good to remember this: most of the time the sorrowful do not need a lot of our words; they need only a little of our compassionate presence.

5. *Bear wrongs patiently.* Jesus told us, "Take up your cross and follow me" (Matthew 16:24). He didn't say, "If you have a cross, take it up." No, he assumed we would have one. This work of mercy reminds us that crosses or "wrongs" are inevitable in life. We should not be surprised or feel guilty, therefore, when we experience them. What are some of our inevitable crosses? Everyday tension, feelings of inadequacy, worry about the future, strains in relationships, to name a few. Bearing wrongs patiently enables us to focus on others' needs rather than be fixated on our own problems.

6. *Forgive all injuries.* This spiritual work of mercy is a "biggie!" It might very well be the most challenging one of all. When it comes to forgiveness, I like what J.V. Taylor said: "Forgiveness grasps the searing stone of sin and will not pass it on." Forgiveness becomes easier if we remember that, in the course of our lifetime, we have hurled a few searing stones at others, too!

7. *Pray for the living and the dead.* Throughout Scripture we are encouraged to pray for others—both the living and the dead. This final spiritual work of mercy, then, is based on the belief in the communion of saints. This means a marvelous bond unites all humankind—both those who have already gone before us into eternal life and those who now share this life on earth with us. This work of mercy encourages us to expand the boundaries of our prayer, which just might expand the boundaries of our love.

Is there any evidence in my life that I practice these spiritual works of mercy?

✚ Loving God, help me to live these spiritual works of mercy in my everyday life.

Modesty

The proud person counts his newspaper clippings—
the humble person his blessings.
—Fulton J. Sheen

Here's a poem I wrote about rice:

Some foods don't mind being cooked in full view:
like eggs frying, pasta boiling, or chicken on the grill.
But not so rice. Rice likes privacy.
It demands a cover while it simmers in the pot,
warning, "No fair peeking till I'm through!"
(And you'd better not, too!)
In a world where privacy is rare,
modesty mocked, and unpretentiousness unheard of,
it's nice to know there are still some things
like rice.

My poem is not really about rice, of course. It is about modesty. Now as soon as I say the word "modesty," some of us immediately think of clothing. We think, modesty is what you do not have if your hemline is too high or your neckline is too low. Or sometimes we equate modesty with shyness or bashfulness. Wallflowers at dances are modest, we say. But modesty is more than how much cleavage you do not show or how far you slink from the dance floor. Modesty is a gift of the Spirit.

The word modesty comes from the Latin word *modestus* which means keeping due measure. Modest people, then, are individuals who keep good measure, that is, they are good at measuring the worth and the extent of things. Their measuring begins with themselves. Modest people have a sense of their own personal worth. This means they know both their talents as well as their limitations. For example, if a good writer says, "I can't write," that is not modesty. That is a lie. But it is not modest for a good writer to say, "My success in writing is totally due to my own self." That too is a lie, for no matter how much talent writers have and no matter how hard they work, they are beholden to a whole host of other factors for their writing success—for example, where they were born, what kind of schooling they had, how healthy they are, what individuals they chanced upon who helped them along the way, and (of course!) their readers.

Modest people also know that not everything has to be made public. Unfortunately, we live in a culture that thrives on publicizing just about everything down to the most intimate details of a person's life. Some of this publicity is uninvited and downright intrusive. But some of it is actually welcomed and cultivated. Someone who seeks such publicity is certainly not modest.

Did Jesus say anything about modesty? Yes, he did. At least indirectly. One reason the Pharisees annoyed Jesus so much was their blatant lack of modesty. For instance, the Pharisees turned personal prayer, which is supposed to be a private matter, into a public spectacle. They gave alms, which were supposed to be given in secret, out in the streets. They even had horns blown when they gave alms to call attention to their charity! And the Pharisees had no sense of their personal limitations. They assumed their religious fervor was the direct result of their efforts alone.

Jesus calls us to modesty. He reminds us of our glory, "You are worth more than many sparrows" (Luke 12:7) and our limitations, "Can you by worrying add a single moment to your life-span?" (Matthew 6:27). He tells us to keep some things private: "When you pray, go to your inner room, close the door, and pray to your Father in secret" (Matthew 6:6). And again, "When you give alms, do not let your left hand know what your right is doing" (Matthew 6:4). Now that is modesty—according to Jesus.

I have a hunch Jesus would like rice, too.

How modest am I? Do I have a good sense of my talents and limitations? Do I have a healthy sense of privacy?

✠ Jesus, help me to go to my inner room, close the door, and pray to God in secret today.

Mystery

It is easier for us to say what God is not, than what God is.
—St. Augustine

In the Old Testament, the Israelites were forbidden to make any images of God. Through Moses, God said to the Israelites, "You saw no form at all on the day the Lord spoke to you at Horeb from the midst of fire. Be strictly on your guard, therefore, not to degrade yourselves by fashioning an idol to represent any figure" (Deuteronomy 4:15).

We Christians who regularly see artistic representations of God as Father, Jesus as Savior, and the Spirit as dove might question the reasoning behind God's prohibition against divine images. After all, don't some images of God actually bring people closer to God? Who, for example, can ever measure the inspiration provided by an ancient icon of the Blessed Trinity or by Michaelangelo's painting of the creation of Adam? What, then, does God have against divine images?

God has only one thing against divine images: they can limit the mystery of God. In other words, we humans could mistake the divine image for divinity itself. In forbidding the Israelites to make an image of God, God was saying to them, "I never want you to confuse a mere image of me with the incomprehensible reality of who I am."

We are as apt to confuse image with reality as the Israelites were, not by bowing down before a golden calf like some of them did. But by bowing down before something else—like nature, for example. That's what pantheists do. They confuse nature with God. They say this sun, this tree, this lake is God—or part of God. And they worship it. Now we might not bow down before a flamingo, but don't we sometimes bow down before other things—like power, money, fame, beauty, success, good health, the latest technology? Don't we sometimes worship these "idols"?

That's where the gift of mystery comes in. A mystery is something that baffles us, something beyond our comprehension. There are mysteries (small letter) and there are Mysteries (capital letter). Small mysteries include things like: "Where's my other sock?...What ever possessed you to do such a thing?... Is there really a Loch Ness monster?" Big Mysteries include things like these: "Why was I born at this time and in this place?...What makes two people fall in love?...Why do bad things happen to good people?" As humans, we tend to be uncomfortable with mysteries. We seem to have this innate need to define, control, and own things. Mysteries, however, refuse to be defined, controlled, and owned by anyone—including us. They elude our manipulation—and this can be good news for our souls.

For every time we encounter mystery, we touch the fringes of God's robe. (I'm speaking metaphorically, of course!) In a way, every mystery we meet helps prepare us for encountering God, the greatest mystery of all. The fact is, the more we know God, the more we know how little we know God. (You might have to read that sentence again.) This sense of God's incomprehensibility was the experience many of the saints had. St. Thomas Aquinas, for example, spent his whole life theologizing and writing about God. His massive *Summa Theologica* has been called the most extensive and systematic exposition of the faith ever written. But toward the end of his life, Thomas had some sort of mystical encounter with God during Mass one day that caused him to retire his pen forever. When questioned why he was no longer writing he said, "I cannot go on....All I have written seems to me like so much straw compared to what I have seen and what has been revealed to me." For Thomas, a whole lifetime of studying and writing about God was nothing compared to one second of actually "seeing" God.

In his book, *The Trivialization of God,* Donald McCullough reminds us how important it is to respect the incomprehensibility of God. The God of Scripture, he says, is not a household pet or warm fuzzy. Rather God is "wholly other, radically different from anything else in creation, terrifying in greatness, and utterly awesome in love."

Yes, mystery is good for the soul. Mystery is also a very good name for God.

How do I experience God's incomprehensibility? Do I ever try to control or manipulate God?

✠ Incomprehensible God, help me to experience your terrifying greatness and your utterly awesome love today.

Patience

Time and I can take on any two.
—Proverb

When I hear the word "saint," the first image that comes to my mind is not some Carmelite nun kneeling in a darkened chapel fingering her rosary beads. Now, I am sure many Carmelite nuns are saints, but they are not the first thing I think of when I hear "saint." Rather, the first image that comes to my mind is a young mother in the parking lot at the mall, trying to get three children—all under five—into their car seats. It reminds me of someone trying to put an octopus to bed.

The woman gets the first child buckled in his seat when the second one starts to scream, "Cookie! Cookie!" The woman digs into a grocery bag, rips open a box of cookies, and shoves one at the kid. Then she lifts him into his car seat. That's when the first kid starts screaming that he wants a cookie, too. She fishes around for a cookie for him. Meanwhile the baby, who is still in the stroller, starts fussing so, after giving a cookie to the first child, the woman turns her attention to the third. That's when the second child starts hitting the first one with the cookie box, and the first one starts to cry. Even when the woman has succeeded, by some miracle, in getting all three children into their car seats, she is not finished yet. She still has to put the shopping bags in the car, collapse the stroller, lift it into the back, and get herself into the car, too. And when she gets home, she has got to reverse the whole process! Now that is great sanctity!

It is also tremendous patience. And patience is yet another gift of the Holy Spirit. The word "patience" is derived from the Latin verb *passio*, meaning to bear or endure. Patient people are those who can bear trials and pains with calmness and equanimity. They are able to put up with delays, wait for the right moment, and bide their time. The great Dominican ecclesiologist, Yves Congar, who saw patience as one of the conditions necessary for authentic church reform, described patience as "a certain disposition of soul and of spirit mindful of necessary delays, a certain humility and pliancy of spirit, the awareness of imperfections, even of inevitable ones."

Patient people are more flexible with time than impatient people. Impatient people exist in only one time frame: their own. They are comfortable with only one schedule: theirs. They want things done when they want things done. And they expect the rest of the world to adapt to their schedule. If they want their child to be potty trained by twenty-four months and he is not by twenty-six, they get angry. If they have to stand in line at the store while an elderly lady ahead of them carries on a brief conversation with the cashier, they get upset because that lady is disrupting their schedule.

Patient people, on the other hand, can flow back and forth between different time frames. They know, for example, that potty training a child may necessitate entering a time frame other than their own. Waiting in line for a few extra moments while an elderly lady chats with a cashier invites patient people to momentarily set aside their own schedule and enter with compassion the schedule of someone else who is lonely and who has more time than she knows what to do with.

Recently I did some creative imaging. I took a walk with Patience. I saw her as an elderly woman in a long white robe and pink slippers. She had short white hair, blue eyes, pink cheeks, and a shy smile which told me she knew a lot more than she was letting on. As we walked together, I found myself always getting ahead of her. She walked more leisurely than I did—strolled is perhaps a more accurate word. I noticed, too, that she made frequent stops along the way to feel the bark of a tree, to talk to the birds, to pet a few mums, and to smile at a child. At the end of our stroll I mustered up enough courage to ask Patience, "What can I do to become more like you?"

She thought for a moment, smiled warmly, and said very slowly, "Plant an acorn...Befriend a turtle...Teach a child."

How patient am I? Am I able to step out of my own time frame and enter with compassion the time frame of someone else?

✠ God of infinite patience, let me stroll with you today.

Piety

*Nowhere does the Torah say, invite your guest to pray, but it
does tell us to offer a guest food, drink, and a bed.*

—Jewish proverb

I used to think a pious person was someone who genuflected profound-
ly before getting into a pew, closed her eyes during prayer, and lit a lot
of candles in church. In other words, piety to me meant the performing
of external religious practices. But then I learned that the scriptural
meaning of "piety" goes far beyond that. It basically means fidelity to
religious duty. And the primary religious duty, of course, is not lighting
candles; it is loving God and our neighbor. True piety does not ask, "Did
you say your prescribed prayers today?" But rather, "How faithful were
you to your duty of loving God and your neighbor?"

In Scripture the word for piety is *hesed* which means compassionate
goodness. *Hesed* is the bond that unites relatives, friends and allies. For
example, *hesed* describes the loving relationship between Jacob and his
sons (Genesis 47:29). It is the bond of friendship between David and
Jonathan (1 Samuel 20:8). And *hesed* is what unites allies. When
Abraham makes a covenant with Abimelech, for instance, he says,
"Swear to me here by God that you will not deal falsely with me or with
my offspring or with my posterity, but as I have dealt loyally with you,
you will deal with me" (Genesis 21:23). That is *hesed.* That is piety.

This human piety is only a faint reflection of God's *hesed,* that is, God's
compassionate goodness toward us. When God makes the covenant with
Israel, God speaks in terms of human piety. To Moses, God says of himself, I am "a merciful and gracious God, slow to anger and rich in kindness and fidelity, continuing (my) kindness for a thousand generations,
and forgiving wickedness and crime and sin" (Exodus 34:6). To the
prophet Jeremiah, God further tells of his *hesed,* "With age-old love I have
loved you; so I have kept my mercy toward you" (Jeremiah 31:3).

God's compassionate goodness toward us calls for a similar response
of love on our part—not only to God, but also to our neighbor. In

Scripture, true piety, therefore, is always associated with justice toward others. Perhaps there is no finer expression of piety than these words of the prophet Micah: "This is what the Lord asks of you: only this, to act justly, to love tenderly, and to walk humbly with your God" (Micah 6:8). Let's look at those three phrases.

To act justly. In their letter "Economic Justice for All," the U.S. Catholic bishops write, "The quest for justice rises from loving gratitude for the saving acts of God and manifests itself in the wholehearted love of God and neighbor." Three words stand out for me in that sentence: quest, gratitude, and wholehearted. The bishops use the phrase "quest for justice," thus reminding us that justice is not something we have already achieved, but something we must continuously strive for. The bishops also say that "justice rises from loving gratitude for the saving acts of God." If we are in touch with the saving acts of God, we will be grateful. It is as simple as that. But we express our gratitude to God not primarily by saying prayers of thanksgiving, but by working for the promotion of justice.

To love tenderly. In their pastoral letter, the bishops also describe the kind of love we are to have for God and neighbor: wholehearted. What does wholehearted love look like? It is a love that is sincere, all-inclusive, enthusiastic, dynamic, impassioned, determined, unreserved. In short, it is the kind of love Jesus showed to the people he ministered to—individuals like the stooped woman, the man with a withered hand, the Roman centurion, the adulterous woman, the little children, the ten lepers, and the multitudes hungry for far more than bread.

To walk humbly with your God. This phrase conjures up images of God walking with Adam and Eve in the garden in the cool of the evening. Or Jesus calmly strolling across the water past his apostles in their boat. Or Jesus nonchalantly hooking up with the two downcast disciples on their way to Emmaus.

The gift of piety, then, does more than light candles. It inflames our hearts.

How faithful am I to my religious duty of loving God and my neighbor?

✝ Loving God, help me to act justly, love tenderly, and walk humbly with you today.

Pleasure

A person will be called to account on Judgment Day for every permissible thing he or she might have enjoyed but did not.
—The Talmud

The poet J. Ruth Gendler has written a delightful book called *The Book of Qualities.* In it she personifies a whole host of familiar words such as: worry, excitement, pain, intuition, truth. She makes each "quality" come alive in a wise and whimsical way. One of my favorite characters in the book is Pleasure. Here is part of Gendler's description:

> Pleasure is wild and sweet. She likes purple flowers…She carries a silver bowl of liquid moonlight…Many people mistrust Pleasure…For a long time I could hardly stand to be in the same room with her…In school we learned she was dangerous, and I was sure she would distract me from my work. I didn't realize she could nurture me.

The description captures the mistrust that some of us have of pleasure. When we hear the word pleasure, we immediately think not of virtue but of sin—more particularly the so-called capital sins: gluttony, lust, sloth. Be honest. When was the last time you heard a sermon proclaiming the merits of bodily pleasures? When was the last time you yourself asked God to increase your capacity for pleasure? Let's face it. When it comes to promoting pleasure, Christianity has a pretty bad track record. We are much more apt to surround pleasure with red flares than we are to present her with red roses.

And that is unfortunate. After all, where did pleasure come from anyway? That's right, from God. God is the ultimate source of all pleasure. (When I taught human sexuality to high school kids, I used to write in big letters on the board: REMEMBER: GOD INVENTED SEX! Sometimes that sentence would blow their minds!)

Jesus scandalized people by eating and drinking too much. His enemies labeled him a glutton, concluding that he enjoyed pleasure too much to be a religious person! A similar story is told about St. Teresa of

Avila, that great mystic and doctor of the Church. It seems her sisters were scandalized one day when they saw Teresa gorging on roast partridge. Sensing their shock, Teresa said to them cheerfully, "At prayer time, pray! At partridge time, partridge!"

How can we grow in our acceptance of and appreciation for pleasure? We can begin by becoming more aware of the built-in pleasures of our daily life. For example, eating is meant to be pleasurable. What can we do to enhance the pleasure of eating? Maybe we need to make time for eating. Rather than zapping boxed meals in the microwave, we could take time to prepare a meal from scratch—at least on a regular basis. Instead of shoving a piece of pizza into our mouths as we race out the door, we could take the time to sit down and eat, savoring our meal— not to mention the company. Maybe it also means eating what is good for us so we do not nullify the pleasure of eating with the pain of indigestion or ill health. Sleep is another pleasure God has invented for us. Do we get enough sleep? Do we deal with problems during the day that might interfere with this pleasure at night?

We might even want to take a "Pleasure Inventory" and list those things that ordinarily bring us pleasure. Here are some of mine: listening to music, playing the piano, phoning a friend, watching birds, swimming, going for a walk, working crossword puzzles, ice skating, playing with a child, reading a good book, hanging out with friends. The list goes on and on. Once we have our list, we can ask ourselves, "When was the last time I did any of these things?" Maybe we have to program pleasure into our pleasure-deprived existence!

One cold February I was feeling depressed. I was dealing with some personal problems at the time, so I attributed my depression to that. But, through a casual conversation with a friend, I suddenly realized I, unknowingly, had not been doing any of those things I really enjoyed doing— those things that gave me pleasure. So what did I do? The next day I laced up my ice-skates and skated on a pond for an hour. It helped. Pleasure can.

What is my basic attitude toward pleasure? What does my "Pleasure Inventory" say to me?

✚ God, source of all pleasure, increase my capacity and appreciation for pleasure.

Prophecy

*The prophets were drunk on God, and in the presence of their terrible
tipsiness, no one was ever comfortable.*
—Frederick Buechner

When we hear the word "prophet," we usually think of someone who predicts the future. Prophets say things like: there's going to be an earthquake in Kalamazoo next Thursday, the Cleveland Indians will win the pennant this year, and tomorrow's winning lotto numbers are 2–6–7. But that's not what prophets did in the Bible. At least, not primarily. In the Bible, a prophet was God's spokesperson, God's mouthpiece. Oh sure, sometimes they said things about the future, but most of the time they talked about the present—which they knew exceptionally well. More often than not, the prophets told people that they were misbehaving and that God was displeased with their misbehaving. As such, prophets had a hard life, for when people are being naughty, the last thing they want to hear is someone telling them they're being naughty.

Most prophets didn't choose to be prophets. They didn't apply for the job. In fact, some went to great lengths to avoid being a prophet. Jonah is perhaps the best example. When God called him to go to Nineveh to prophesy, Jonah promptly made a 180-degree turn and ran away. But God caught up with him eventually, because God was on a first-name basis with a certain whale. When God called Moses, Moses came up with all kinds of creative excuses why he couldn't be a prophet—everything short of, "But I've got bad breath!" But Moses, too, eventually caved in and took the job. At one point the prophet Jeremiah tried with all his heart to stop prophesying, but he just couldn't keep his mouth or his heart shut.

The prophets' reluctance to prophesy stemmed from the fact that prophecy was a dangerous profession, one that merited this label: WARNING: Prophesying can be hazardous to your health! The prophets, as a rule, were treated terribly. Jeremiah was thrown into a cistern. Elijah was chased hither and yon by the wicked queen Jezebel. His life became so unbearable, he begged God for death on more than one occasion. But God always said, "Not yet."

In addition to being reluctant, the prophets were also a little strange. Let's face it, they weren't the type of individuals you'd invite to your dinner party. Some, like John the Baptist, ate bugs and never combed their hair. Ezekiel was worse. Once he ate a book! Then he had the audacity to say it tasted just like honey! And poor Jeremiah was always doing weird things—like walking around wearing the yoke of an ox around his neck and smashing perfectly good clay pots in the town square.

But despite their idiosyncrasies, the prophets were a courageous lot. Take the prophet Nathan. He had the gall to tell King David to his face that he was a cheat, a liar, an adulterer, and a murderer! David was really all those things, too, but, fortunately for Nathan, he was also repentant. Instead of killing Nathan on the spot, David admitted his sins and turned his life around. All thanks to the courageous prophet.

Jesus was something of a prophet although he never claimed the title for himself. He did some strange things—like giving up a fairly secure job as a carpenter to become an itinerant preacher with no pay. He was God's mouthpiece calling people to repentance and assuring them of God's unfailing love. He was courageous, standing up to opposition even when he needed no crystal ball to see where it was leading him. And, of course, Jesus suffered immeasurably—probably more than any of the prophets before him.

What does prophecy have to do with us? What does this motley group of individuals and the prophesying Jesus teach us? We may not eat bugs or smash clay pots, but we are called to be in touch with our times (see the chapters on PIETY and TRUTH). Like the prophets, we can also offer advice when we are asked and not act as if we haven't learned anything from our own prayer and experience that might be helpful to others. And we can also imitate the prophets' ability to console and encourage others, for that, too, was one of their major tasks. And finally, we, like the prophets, can care. We can care about our families, friends, community, parish, church, and world. Care enough to speak God's truth.

Do I always speak the truth even when it is hard to do so? Whom have I consoled and encouraged lately?

✠ Spirit of Jesus, fill me with your truth.

Relaxation

The challenge of being human is so great, no one gets it right every time.
—Rabbi Harold Kushner

One of my favorite cartoons shows two snakes. One is resting on the ground, his body relaxed in supple curves. The other is leaning against a tree, his body stiff and straight as a board. The one on the ground says to the other, "Charlie, you've gotta learn to relax already!" Many of us need to hear those same words, "Relax already!" We might be more inclined to do so, too, if we were really convinced that relaxation is, indeed, a gift of the Holy Spirit. This chapter will try to convince you.

Let's begin by looking at the main enemy of relaxation: perfectionism. Many people cannot relax because they are trying too hard to be perfect. Perfectionists are people who put excessive demands upon themselves and sometimes upon others as well. Psychiatrists say that perfectionism is often a way of compensating for low self-esteem. It can also arise from repressed fears of abandonment or shame.

In her book, *Bird By Bird,* Anne Lamott calls perfectionism "the voice of the oppressor." She continues, "Perfectionism is based on the obsessive belief that if you run carefully enough, hitting each stepping-stone just right, you won't have to die." She concludes, "The truth is you will die anyway and a lot of people who aren't even looking at their feet are going to do a lot better than you, and have a lot more fun while they're doing it."

Both perfectionism and our ability to relax are directly linked to our image of God. If we believe God is out to get us and is sitting up in heaven with a clipboard, carefully noting our every failing, then we can easily become perfectionists. If, on the other hand, we believe God loves us immensely and is walking beside us, whispering in our ear, "Don't be afraid. Nothing can happen that you and I can't handle together," then we can readily afford to relax.

Jesus knew how to relax. He frequented the home of Mary, Martha, and Lazarus, for example, not to preach to them, but to relax with them.

In their home in Bethany, Jesus was able to kick his feet up and let his hair down. We sense Jesus knew how to relax, too, when we read his parables. How did he come up with such effective images for his parables—bread rising, seeds germinating, camels squeezing through narrow gates, wayward sons returning home—except that he took the time to observe the world around him, to converse with people, and to reflect upon his own lived experience. He could do that, because he knew how to relax.

Not only did Jesus relax himself, he also told his disciples to relax, too, on numerous occasions. "Come away by yourselves to a deserted place and rest a while," he said to the twelve when they returned from their exhausting speaking engagements (Mark 6:31). And other times he said to his listeners things like, "Don't worry...don't be afraid...stop fretting." Why? "Because God loves you like there's no tomorrow." And "Because everything ultimately is in God's hands."

The philosopher Immanuel Kant wrote, "Out of timber as crooked as that which (we are) made of, nothing perfectly straight can be carved." Yes, we are made of crooked timber. Can we give up the vain hope that something perfectly straight can be carved from us? Can we even give up the belief that the perfectly straight is an ideal to strive for? Can we accept our crookedness? More than that, can we embrace our warps, our splinters, and our knotholes? And finally, can we trust that the Divine Woodcarver will, in the end, fashion each of us into a magnificent work of art? If we can say "yes" to all these questions, then surely we can relax already!

In his classic book entitled, *Leisure: the Basis of Culture,* Josef Pieper wrote: "Unless we regain the art of silence and insights, the ability of non-activity, unless we substitute true leisure for our hectic amusements, we will destroy our culture—and ourselves." Those words were written almost fifty years ago. They still are true today.

Am I ever a perfectionist? What helps me to relax?

✝ Holy Spirit, bless me with the grace to relax today!

Responsibility

If not us, who? If not now, when?
—Slogan of Czech University students in Prague, 1989

In his book, *A World of Stories for Preachers and Teachers,* William Bausch tells this little-known fact about riding in a stagecoach in the old West. The stagecoach had three kinds of tickets: first class, second class, and third class. If you had a first class ticket, you were allowed to remain seated the entire trip no matter what happened. If the stagecoach got stuck in the mud, or had trouble going up a steep hill, or even if one of its wheels fell off, you could remain seated. If you had a second class ticket, you could remain seated until there was a problem. In that case, you had to get off the stagecoach until the problem was solved. You could stand around and watch as others fixed the problem. You yourself did not have to actually get your hands dirty. And as soon as the problem was fixed, you were allowed to get back into your seat. If you had a third class ticket, you had to get off the stagecoach if there was a problem because it was your responsibility to help fix the problem. This means you had to get out and push the stagecoach out of the mud or up the hill, or even help fix a broken wheel.

After hearing this, we might ask ourselves, "On the stagecoach journey of life, what kind of ticket am I holding?" First class? That means if there is a problem, I do nothing about it. In fact, others have to work around me. A second class ticket? That means I watch others try to fix life's problems. Or a third class ticket? This means I sense it is partly my responsibility to help fix the problems encountered along the journey of life.

I believe that we, as Christians, hold third class tickets on the stagecoach of life, that is, we are called to help solve life's problems. In fact, assuming that responsibility is what discipleship is all about.

We see this by looking at the gospels. When Jesus calls his disciples, he invites them not merely to be with him and enjoy his company. Rather, he calls them to observe what he does and to learn from him, so they too might share in his work. Each of the gospels makes this point very clear. In Mark, for example, the evangelist spends five chapters describing the ministry of Jesus in considerable detail. Jesus cures the sick, casts out devils, and teaches the crowds. Then Jesus does something incredible: he sends the disciples off to do the same wonderful works that he has done: "So they went off and preached repentance. They drove out demons, and they anointed with oil many who were sick and cured them" (Mark 6:12–13).

Jesus entrusts his disciples with responsibility at the end of his life, too. At the ascension, he says to his disciples, "Go, therefore, and make disciples of all nations, baptizing them in the name of the Father, and of the Son, and of the Holy Spirit, teaching them to observe all that I have commanded you" (Matthew 28:19–20). Talk about responsibility! Fortunately, Jesus adds these consoling words, "And behold, I am with you always, until the end of the age" (Matthew 28:20).

The big question to ask ourselves is this: for what or for whom do I feel responsible? Some people feel responsible only for themselves. This excessive individualism is in the very air that we breathe. Other individuals feel responsible only for their immediate family or their little circle of friends. The rest of the world can go to pot as far as they're concerned. Still others feel responsible only for their local community, their parish, their particular ethnic group. They see no connection between their local community, for instance, and the larger global community.

But through the gift of responsibility, the Spirit is forever trying to enlarge the sweep of our love, reminding us that we are part of something more important than our individual selves, more expansive than our family circle or particular ethnic group. We are members of a community, a church, a nation, a world. As such, we must continuously work to further the coming of God's Kingdom. That is our responsibility. That is our call.

For what or to whom do I have a responsibility? How may the Spirit be calling me to expand the sweep of my love?

✚ Jesus, help me to see more clearly my responsibility for furthering God's Kingdom in my time and place!

Song

"How can I keep from singing?"
—Traditional Hymn

A number of years ago when I was novice director, I had a novice, Sister Liz, who liked to sing. She sang often, not loudly or annoyingly, but quietly and unobtrusively as she went about her chores like folding laundry or mopping the floor. I liked to hear Liz sing, and I soon dubbed her "radio station WLIZ." Her gentle song lifted my own spirits and assured me that things were going well for her. (I'm happy to report, that station WLIZ is still on the air!)

I myself like to sing, too. Little wonder, then, that I was struck by something I read a while back. It said, of all the commands God gave to the Israelites, the most frequently repeated one was "Sing!" I was surprised. I would have guessed a command like repent, believe, remember, trust, or forgive. Yet little "sing" outnumbers them all. We see this command of God reflected throughout the psalms: *"Sing* joyfully to God our strength" (Psalm 81:2) and "O Come let us *sing* joyfully to our God" (Psalm 95:1). Why was God so intent on commanding the Israelites (and us!) to sing?

Aldous Huxley wrote, "After silence, that which comes nearest to expressing the inexpressible is music." Maybe God commanded the Israelites to sing because song or music is so much like God, the Inexpressible One. Have you ever noticed in the Bible how God and song go hand in hand? Whenever God pays a visit to people in Scripture, they often end up singing. For example, when God parted the Red Sea, and the Israelites marched through it without a trace of mud on their sandals, what was the first thing they did? That's right, they sang: "Then Moses and the Israelites sang this song to the Lord: I will sing to the Lord, for he is gloriously triumphant; horse and chariot he has cast into the sea" (Exodus 15:1). When Hannah (see the chapter on WHIMSY) gave birth to little Samuel, the answer to her prayer, she too broke out in song: "My heart exults in the Lord, my horn is exalted in my God" (1 Samuel 2:1). When Mary visited Elizabeth, she sang her famous aria, the Magnificat: "The mighty One has done great things for me, and holy is his name" (Luke 1:49). It's as if, when we humans detect that God is near, we can't help but break out into song.

Strictly speaking, God is the origin of all song. It is safe to say, then, our affinity for song is one of the ways we are made in God's image and likeness. In fact, it is easy for me to imagine God *singing* creation into being. I can picture God belting out the commands in a robust baritone voice—or a rich alto voice: "Let there be light!...Let there be oceans!...Let there be porcupines!" Conversely, I suspect that the devil is someone who cannot sing—that with his fall from grace, he lost the gift of song. And what a loss that is! Perhaps a good description of hell is the place where no one sings and where no flute is ever heard.

Jesus probably sang. Like most children of his time, he would have learned his first songs from his parents. We can imagine Jesus going to the synagogue as a child, and listening with rapt attention (or squirming with childish impatience) at the canting of the sacred texts during Sabbath prayer. As an adult, Jesus, in all likelihood, did not merely recite the psalms, he probably sang them—as they were meant to be prayed. And at the Last Supper, it is not far-fetched at all to suppose that Jesus sang even the sacred words we now use at the consecration: "This is my body....this is my blood...do this in memory of me."

The poet Carlyle said music was the "speech of angels." Longfellow too saw a direct link between faith and song. He called song "the Prophet's art," and added that "Among the gifts that God hath sent," music is "one of the most magnificent." It is only fitting, then, that we conclude this reflection on the gift of song with this melodic message of the prophet, Isaiah, who said (or perhaps sang) these words: "The Lord is my salvation. The Lord is my strength and my song" (Isaiah 12:2).

What role do song and music play in my life? In my prayer?

✚ God, Source of all music, make my life a song for you!

Stability

Stability has far more to do with honesty than it does with one's zip code.
—Demetrius Dumm, OSB

When I was a little girl, I sometimes misbehaved. (People who know me well will not be surprised.) When I was bad, my mother had an effective way of disciplining me. She did not scream or spank me. Instead, she pointed to one of the chairs in the dining room and said, "Sit! Until I tell you you can move." Now sitting still in one place was pure torture for me. Although I seldom had to sit there for more than a few minutes, those few minutes dragged on and on until I was sure I had been sitting on that chair for a hundred years! Sometimes, if I detected my mother was in a negotiable mood, I would plead with her to please let me get off the chair, adding with as much sincerity as I could muster, "I'll be good! I promise!"

Staying in one place is hard not only for children, but also for adults. We humans have an innate affinity for movement. Isn't this why babies like to be rocked, why we find cars so appealing, and why we can stare for hours at a river flowing by? So, when I say stability is one of the gifts of the Spirit, some might say, "You're kidding, aren't you?" No, I am not kidding. But first let's explore what stability as a gift of the Spirit really means.

To begin, I turn to my old friend, Father Demetrius Dumm, OSB, author of *Cherish Christ Above All*, a book on the rule of St. Benedict. As some may know, Benedictines actually take a vow of stability. In his book, Dumm explains the reason behind this practice. He begins by describing Benedict's attitude toward the wandering monks of his day. Benedict called them "gyrovagues." These were monks who spent their entire lives drifting from place to place, staying for only three or four days in different monasteries. Says Benedict, "Always on the move, they never settle down, and are slaves to their own wills and gross appetites."

Benedict saw a danger in such "instability." By flitting from monastery to monastery, these monks never allowed others to get to know them. Consequently, they never really learned to know themselves. As Dumm says, "Benedict wants his followers to stay in one place, where others can get to know them well, and where these others will, in various ways, enable them to learn the truth about themselves." Dumm explains why this kind of truth is so critical for the spiritual life: "because real spiritual growth can occur only when one begins with honest self-knowledge."

Stability, then, does not simply mean staying in one place—although it can include that. More accurately, however, it means not running away from the self-knowledge we can gain only through interaction with others. We will be tempted to run away, too, because self-knowledge can hurt. Over the years, I have devised a little practice that helps me deal with the pain of self-knowledge. When, usually through interaction with others, I come face to face with a shortcoming of mine, I say to myself, "Ouch!" In other words, "Ouch! I'm not as kind as I thought I was...Ouch! I'm not as responsible as I imagined...Ouch! I'm not as loving as I assumed." For some strange reason, saying ouch to myself lessens the pain of the moment— much like a woman who (more intensely, of course!) screams during child-birth. The childbirth analogy, by the way, is a good one, for every moment of honest self-knowledge can, indeed, be a moment of birth.

But self-knowledge is not always painful. Sometimes it is downright pleasurable. For honest self-knowledge also includes those good things about ourselves that we sometimes learn only from others: "You're really thoughtful...I get a kick out of you...I admire your courage...Thanks for making me laugh." Stability prevents us from running away from our virtues as well as our vices. It means never brushing off a compliment, either.

Rabbi Hillel, a first-century Jewish teacher, gave this advice: "Do not withdraw from community." Stability is the gift that keeps us rooted in community and, as such, rooted in the truth of who we are.

Do I ever run away from the self-knowledge I can gain only through inter-action with others? Do I brush off compliments?

✚ God, give me the gift of stability that I may more willingly grow in self-knowledge.

Surrender

Surrender is yielding to God's dream for us.
—James Krisher

For many of us, the word "surrender" conjures up only negative images. We see a cowardly cowboy raising a white handkerchief on a stick. Or we recall being pinned to the living room floor by an older sibling and forced to cry "Uncle!" Even the synonyms we use for "surrender" reinforce this negativity: to give up, to abandon, to buckle under, to hand over, to eat humble pie, to cave in, to quit.

Another reason the word "surrender" is so pejorative is because of the highly competitive society in which we live. It is forever telling us that winning is everything. It teaches us to control, dominate and (above all) never give up! Even if we do not see surrender as cowardly, we tend to view it as essentially passive. Surrender means to accept things as they are, to go with the flow, to adopt a *que sera, sera* attitude. If all of this is true, then how in the world can we say that surrender is a gift of the Holy Spirit?

Let me answer that question by telling a brief story. Suppose a six-year-old boy gets mad at his parents for not buying him a pony. In anger, he runs away from home and hides in the neighbor's backyard shed. As darkness descends and the temperature begins to plummet, he hears the frantic cries of his parents calling his name. What can he do? He could remain shivering in the shed all night long and perhaps get sick or even freeze to death. Or he could come out of his hiding place and surrender to his parents. Assuming his parents are basically good parents, what would be the best thing for the boy to do? That's right, to surrender. Surrender, then, although it is sometimes a negative thing, can also be a very positive act. It all depends on what or whom you are surrendering to. If we surrender ourselves to drugs or alcohol, our surrender is certainly not a good thing. But if we surrender ourselves to treatment for drug or alcohol abuse, then our surrender is a wonderful thing.

James Krisher has written a book entitled *Spiritual Surrender: Yielding*

Yourself to a Loving God. In it, he says that spiritual surrender, that is, yielding to God, is anything but wimpish or passive. In fact, spiritual surrender takes great courage and resolve. Krisher gives a fine description of such surrender as "an active choice to place our person, forces, and possessions into the hands of God." Such surrender is always life-giving.

To place our person, forces and possessions into God's hands. Our faith tradition is replete with individuals who surrendered to God in that fashion and, by doing so, found abundant new life not only for themselves, but for others. Moses surrendered to God at the burning bush and went on to deliver the Israelites from slavery. Jonah surrendered to God in the belly of the whale and saved the Ninevites from destruction. Mary surrendered to God at the annunciation and gave birth to the Messiah. Paul surrendered to God on the road to Damascus and became the great apostle to the Gentiles. Ignatius surrendered to God on a hospital bed and went on to found a congregation that has served the church for over 450 years. Sojourner Truth surrendered to God in 1843 and became one of the most influential voices against the evils of slavery.

Spiritual surrender is not always easy or neat. It is seldom once-and-for-all, either. Our God is a God who calls us again and again. Like a persistent lover, God pursues, charms, and woos us. The prophet Jeremiah experienced firsthand the irresistible attractiveness of God. He describes his own spiritual surrender in these memorable words: "Oh Lord, you have enticed me, and I was enticed; you have overpowered me, and you have prevailed" (Jeremiah 20:7).

It is my guess that those of you reading this book have already experienced something of spiritual surrender. Hopefully, having tasted the new life that such surrender brings, you (like me) desire only this: to surrender ever more completely to our God, the Divine Lover.

Have I ever experienced spiritual surrendering? What holds me back from surrendering completely to God?

✠ God, you have enticed me. Help me to surrender more completely to your dream for me.

Truth

The truth will set you free.
—John 8:32

Here is the truth about truth.

Truth is not the same as facts. How tall I am, how much a ring costs, and what I ate for supper last night are all facts. But truth goes deeper than facts. It includes things like how I feel about my height, what value the ring has for me personally, and why I had what I had for supper last night. Facts tell us what things are. Truth reveals to us what things mean.

There are many kinds of truth: mathematical, scientific, theological, philosophical, poetic, psychological. Truth can never be limited to just one of these kinds. Nor can one kind of truth be held superior to another. There can be just as much truth in a poem, for instance, as there is in a scientific formula. Ultimately, truth is all of these kinds of truth together. Also, truth can go wherever she wants. She can show up in a science lab, a church, a courtroom, an assembly line, a classroom, a bedroom—provided she is invited. Sometimes she even shows up uninvited. Although truth is comfortable with everyone, she seems especially at home with children and the dying.

Truth is not always obvious. She tends to be shyer than deceit, more reserved than dishonesty. Truth is far more careful and attentive than inaccuracy, too. That's one reason she gets around more slowly than falsehood. As Mark Twain said, "A lie can travel around the world before the truth even puts on her shoes!" Some people are strangers to truth; others are bosom friends with her. But still, no one knows her completely. As the old proverb warns, "Align yourself with the person who seeks the truth, but run away from the one who claims to have found it!"

We do not always see the truth clearly. Sometimes that's because the truth is difficult to decipher, yes. But more often than not, it is because we are more comfortable not seeing her. For truth can sting or hurt—terribly. So we say things like, "There's nothing wrong with my marriage…My kid is not on drugs…I am not lonely…Everything's fine!" To admit otherwise would inflict pain too great for us to bear—or so we imagine. If only we would realize that, ultimately, the pain that truth brings is never as great as the pain of living without her. What's more, truth's pain is only temporary. It eventually leaves, making room for the other friends truth always brings with her: humility, trust, forgiveness, and freedom.

St. Thomas Aquinas said that falsehood is never so false as when it is nearly true. It is never so dangerous either. For, a near truth (or a half truth) can inflict far more damage than a whole lie. That's because we are taken in more easily by a half truth than a complete falsehood. Selfish people, for example, defend their selfishness by saying, "I am important." That is true. But only half true. The other half of that truth is "So is everyone else." Some countries, like the United States, have been known to proclaim another half truth: "God has blessed our land with many natural resources." The other part of that truth is, "God wants us to share those resources with the rest of the world."

From the onset of his public ministry, Jesus aligned himself firmly with truth. He spoke the truth even when it meant a loss of popularity. He repeatedly denounced truth's opposites—especially pride and hypocrisy. Ultimately, he identified his very self with truth when he said, "I am the way, the truth, and the life" (John 14:6). Jesus went to his death with the truth upon his lips, refusing to deny who he really was. Pilate asked him, "Are you a king then?" He answered, "Yes, I am a king" (John 18:33–37). And they led him away to be crucified.

In the end, there are these two: love and truth, standing together, their arms forever linked. Neither can live without the other. For truth without love is empty. And love without truth is an illusion.

This is the truth about truth. But, of course, not all the truth.

What has been my experience of truth? Have I ever experienced her pain or her freedom?

✚ Jesus, you are the Truth. Help me to align myself with truth today and every day.

Understanding

Jesus summoned the crowd and said to them, "Hear and understand."
—Matthew 15:10

If you were on trial for your life, what kind of people would you want on your jury? Honest? Attentive? Responsible? Fair? If you had to pick only one quality that all of them would have, what quality would you choose? I know which one I would choose: understanding.

Understanding is the ability to crawl into another person's skin. It means to walk a mile in their moccasins (or high heels or sandals or sneakers or cowboy boots or bare feet!). It means to see things from their perspective, to sense how they feel. Understanding is a close relative of compassion. In fact, it is often difficult to tell where one ends and the other begins. I, for one, think understanding usually arrives first on the scene. It says, "Oh, now I see! Now I understand!" Compassion comes immediately after and says, "Now that I understand, I feel very deeply and I want to help!" (see the chapter on COMPASSION). Like compassion, understanding is not easy to arrive at. In fact, it demands considerable asceticism—especially the asceticism of detachment and humility.

Understanding demands detachment. It means I must let go of my own way of looking at things—at least temporarily—in order to take up someone else's way of perceiving reality. If I am Tom, a middle-aged white man in Boston, and I'm trying to understand Latisha, a young African-American woman in Atlanta, then I must let go of my middle-agedness, my whiteness, my maleness, and even Boston to begin to understand Latisha. If Latisha wants to understand Tom, then she must do the same kind of letting go. This is no small feat. In fact, some would argue that it is downright impossible to let go of so much in order to embrace another's reality. Understanding understands this, but still says, "Try it! Make the effort at least! Take one baby step toward knowing and appreciating another, and you'll see, you'll see!"

Understanding requires humility. It concedes, "My perception is incomplete. My world is not the whole world. There are other ways of doing things, other values and experiences that are just as valid as my own." And understanding means it, too.

The opposite of understanding is a judgmental attitude. Understanding needs time. Judgmental people, on the other hand, are usually in a rush. Rather than take the time to get to know people, they take the shortcut and judge them. Judgmental people are not only in a hurry, they are often fearful, too. The prospect of letting go of their world—their ideas, opinions, habits, and value systems—terrifies them. Besides, they find it hard to understand why anyone would ever want to do such a thing. And finally, judgmental individuals sometimes lack imagination. This makes it hard for them to envision how others think or feel. (I hope I haven't been too judgmental of judgmental people!)

Jesus was understanding. We know this in several ways. First, he was exceptionally approachable. Though a male Jew, he was readily approached not only by other male Jews, but also by women, children, and Gentiles. Tradition says his background was probably carpentry, yet he gave ample evidence of understanding the world of fishermen, farmers, builders, merchants, and housewives. Although in good health, he understood the plight of the sick. Jesus was slow to judge. Even a woman caught in the act of adultery did not merit his condemnation. He readily forgave people—even those who had wronged him personally. While hanging on the cross he forgave his executioners. When, after the resurrection, he encountered his unfaithful apostles, he extended his hand in forgiveness. Jesus could so readily forgive others precisely because he was so understanding. He could imagine what made people do some of the terrible things they did.

The gift of understanding is sorely needed in a world such as ours, a world marked by excessive individualism, growing mistrust, accelerating violence, and "ism's" of all kinds—racism, nationalism, sexism, ageism. As such, the gift of understanding plays not a cameo role in our lives as Christians. Rather it has a leading role in bringing about the Kingdom of God here on earth. If only we would understand that better!

What evidence do I give of having received the gift of understanding? Is there any evidence that I am judgmental?

✚ God of Understanding, help me to crawl into someone else's skin today.

Whimsy

If it looks like fun and doesn't break the Ten Commandments, do it.
—Karol A. Jackowski

A neighbor was telling me about her friend in a nursing home. "Florence is a good woman," she said. "A little pixilated, but good." I had not heard the word "pixilated" in a long time. I knew what it meant in general—slightly unbalanced mentally, in a harmless sort of way. But when I got home, I looked the word up in the dictionary, and found it literally means "to be visited by pixies," those cheerful, mischievous little elves. One of the synonyms for pixilation was whimsy, which I like to think of as one of the gifts of the Holy Spirit.

Whimsy can mean several things. It can mean something fanciful or odd. Often the word connotes unpredictable behavior or erratic change. The word is most appropriate for religious discussions, for it captures what can happen when God pays us a visit. We become whimsical. That is, we are changed. Our behavior becomes unpredictable. We may even be thought odd or mentally unbalanced by others.

Scripture presents us with a slew of whimsical people. But one of my favorites is Hannah, the mother of Samuel (1 Samuel 1:1–23). Hannah is married to Elkanah who has another wife named Peninnah. Hannah is as barren as a rock, whereas Peninnah is as fertile as a turtle. Day after day Peninnah mocks Hannah for her barrenness. We can almost hear her taunting, "Nah! Nah! Nah! Nah! Nah!" and see her sticking her tongue out. Poor Elkanah must have had his hands full. But the story says that he clearly favors Hannah despite her childlessness.

Year after year, Hannah makes a pilgrimage to the sanctuary of the Lord, begging God to send her a son. But to no avail. Or so it seems. Then one day, she goes to the sanctuary and throws herself on the floor, flooding the place with her tears. Rocking back and forth, like one being visited by more than pixies, she cries in her heart to God, "If you give me a son, I'll give him right back to you, to serve you in the temple. I promise!" What a whimsical thing to say!

Eli, a priest of God, sees Hannah groveling in the sanctuary. He thinks, "That woman's plastered!" and stomps over to restore respectability to this holy place. Shaking his bony finger at her, he scolds her severely. But Hannah explains the reason for her strange behavior, sharing with him the agony from which her tears and wailing proceed. Eli, himself well acquainted with pain, listens attentively and tells her finally, "Go in peace. And may God grant you your request." That's all Hannah needs to hear. She picks herself up, goes home and, after a few nights of lovemaking with Elkanah (the Bible is very clear about that!), she conceives a child. Finally! Nine months later she gives birth to Samuel.

But as soon as little Sammie is weaned, Hannah plops him in his stroller, packs him a suitcase, grabs her husband, and they all march off to the temple to make the customary offering to God. But when it comes time to leave, Hannah does the seemingly impossible thing: she hands her son to Eli, saying, "Here, he's yours." Or, more accurately, "Here, he's God's." In other words, she gives her son to the service of God in the temple—as she had promised even before she had conceived him. Isn't that strange? Isn't that odd? She who begged and begged for a son and now had him, was giving him up! Talk about whimsy! But the best whimsy is yet to come.

As Hannah and Elkanah exit the temple, Hannah is visited by more than pixies again. She is filled with the spirit of God and sings out a magnificent hymn of thanksgiving to God. "My heart exults in the Lord," she cries. Then she proceeds to describe a world made topsy-turvy by a God who seems to delight in surprise and the unexpected. "The bows of the mighty are broken, while the tottering gird on strength. The well-fed hire themselves out for bread, while the hungry fatten on spoil." On and on this possessed woman goes singing the praises of a whimsical God who refuses to be held back by the limits of our human expectations.

Many years later, another woman, full of whimsy too, will echo Hannah's words. Only her child will not be an ordinary child. He will be the Son of God.

Do I have any whimsy? Have I ever been visited by the whimsical God?

✚ God of whimsy, visit me and break through the limits of my human expectations.

Wisdom

When wisdom enters, subtlety comes along.
—Talmud

Recently I came across these words of wisdom written by little children:

1. When your mom is mad at your dad, don't let her brush your hair.
2. You can't trust dogs to watch your food.
3. Never confuse a crayon with a Tootsie Roll.
4. The best place to be when you're sad is in Grandma's lap.

Wisdom is the gift of the Spirit that tells us how to live. It reveals to us the nature of reality and directs us to live our lives in accord with that reality. Wisdom tells us what is true, right, and lasting. It helps us to discern values, enter into relationships, and make good judgments.

But there are different kinds of wisdom. One kind is human wisdom or conventional wisdom. Human wisdom says things like: Love your friends, but hate your enemies...The important thing is the bottom line...Winning is everything. But Christians believe in a wisdom derived from the teachings of Jesus. This wisdom says: Love your friends and your enemies...The important thing is compassion...Loving, not winning, is everything. In short, not everything that looks like wisdom really is.

This idea is brought out in Marcus Borg's book, *Meeting Jesus Again for the First Time*. Borg devotes two chapters to a discussion of Jesus and wisdom. He begins by saying that Jesus was above all a teacher of wisdom, a sage. But Jesus' wisdom was often in opposition to the conventional wisdom of his day. We can see this in Jesus' aphorisms (those great one-liners) and in his parables (those great short stories).

The gospels record over a hundred of Jesus' aphorisms. For example: "You cannot serve two masters"; "The last shall be first"; "You strain out a gnat and swallow a camel"; "If a blind person leads a blind person, will they not both fall into a ditch?" All of his aphorisms invite his listeners to see something in a new way. As Borg says, "they tease the imagination into activity, suggest more than they say, and invite a transformation of perception." We might add, Jesus' aphorisms lead to a new kind of wisdom.

Let's look at one of those aphorisms: "You strain out a gnat and swallow a camel." These words were directed toward the Pharisees who emphasized legal purity in a big way. Though the image is humorous, the point is serious: how foolish it is to strain out something teeny weeny while swallowing something humongous. Jesus' words invite his listeners (and us!) to raise questions such as these: Do I ever do something as foolish as this? What are the gnats and camels in my life? What is the relationship between religious practices and religion itself?

Another way Jesus set forth his wisdom was through his parables. Notice, however, that Jesus did not force his wisdom onto anyone. In fact, he often began his stories with phrases like these: "Judge for yourself what is right" or "What do you think?" As Borg says, his style of delivery "was invitational rather than imperative." One parable that starkly contradicts conventional wisdom is the story of the workers in the vineyard (Matthew 20:1–16). As you recall, the workers come to the vineyard at various times during the day. Some arrive early in the morning, others do not show up until noon, and a third group shuffles in at the last minute. Yet, at the end of the day, when the workers file by to get their wages, the owner of the vineyard pays them all the same amount. The workers who slaved all day are outraged, of course. (And so too are many of us!) This parable raises questions about our understanding of justice, our motivation for working, and the nature of God's love. It, like so many other parables of Jesus, proclaims: "Your human wisdom is not necessarily God's wisdom."

For Christians, the ultimate wisdom, of course, is the folly of the cross. St. Paul says this well when he writes to the Corinthians, "Has not God made the wisdom of the world foolish?...But we proclaim Christ crucified, a stumbling block to [many]...For the foolishness of God is wiser than human wisdom" (1 Corinthians 1:20, 23, 25).

What are some ways the wisdom of Jesus is in opposition to the wisdom of our day? To what extent have I embraced the folly of the cross?

✝ Jesus, Sage of God, fill me with your wisdom.

Wishing

Sometimes wishing is the wings the truth comes true on.
—Frederick Buechner

When I taught high school religion, sometimes a student would ask me, "What if Jesus was a hoax? What if he never even existed? What if there isn't any God, and all this stuff we're learning is one big fat lie? Then what?"

Good question. It is one I have asked myself on more than one occasion, too. In fact, I have also asked, "What if this whole nun thing is wrong? What if my vows—especially celibacy—have all been for naught? Then what?"

I have several ways of responding to that "Then what?" I ask myself, "Well, have you been basically happy believing in Jesus and Christianity?" My answer: Yes! "Have you been basically happy living the life of a nun?" Again, my answer is yes! "Have you brought happiness to others by living a life based on Christian principles?" Again, I believe so. And finally, "What have you *lost* by believing in Jesus, by embracing Christianity?" Well, I am not sure. I have a hunch I have lost some money. And I know for sure I have lost a lot of time. Just think of all the extra time I would have had if I had never prayed, never gone to church, never read a spiritual book, or never served others.

The point is, of course, we do not know for sure about Jesus or Christianity. If we did, we would have no need for faith. Certainty rules out faith. Furthermore, one reason I stick with Christianity is not because I am absolutely sure it is true, but rather because I have found such happiness and fulfillment in living a life based upon its principles. And I admire the lives of so many other people who have also staked their claim on the gospel. In addition, I say this: if Christianity is not true, then I wish with all my heart that it would be true. If Jesus is only a figment of someone's imagination, then what a marvelous figment he is! If his teachings about God's unfailing love for us, charity's universal application (even to one's enemies), goodness' ultimate triumph over evil, and life's final victory over death, are only a story, then what a splendid story it is!

Frederick Buechner has written an intriguing little book entitled *Wishful Thinking: A Theological ABC*. Dubbed "a dictionary for the restless believer," the book is a collection of imaginative and thought-provoking definitions of many traditional Christian terms—such as angels, the cross, idolatry, meditation, and sin. In the book, Beuchner defines "wishful thinking" like this: "Christianity is mainly wishful thinking. Even the part about Judgment and Hell reflect the wish that somewhere the score is being kept." Then he adds, "Sometimes the Truth is what sets us wishing for it."

I like that sentence. To me it says that our very capacity for wishing comes from God. It is God, Truth itself, who has set our hearts to wishing in the first place. (By the way, we sometimes call this wishing "hope.") What are we wishing or hoping for? For all kinds of things like peace, love, harmony, joy, excitement, understanding, meaning. And our very wishing for such things can be the first step toward making them a reality.

Martin Luther King, Jr. was a man who wasn't afraid of wishing. Poised on the steps of the Lincoln Memorial in the summer of 1963, he cried out: "I have a dream!" He could just as easily have said, "I have a wish!" or "I have this incredible hope!" And he shared his dream—his wish, his hope—with the 200,000 people gathered there that day, and with millions of others who continue to be inspired by his words. It was King's dream that created the momentum that resulted in the passage of the Civil Rights Act of 1964, an act that was a major step toward making King's wish come true.

One of my favorite images of hope comes from Sister Macrina Widerkehr, OSB, who wrote, "I was just thinking one morning during meditation how much alike hope and baking powder are: quietly getting what is best in me to rise, awakening the hint of eternity within."

What am I wishing for?

✚ God, may I encounter your truth in all my wishes today.

Zeal

Nothing great in the world has ever been
accomplished without enthusiasm.
—Georg Hegel

I tend to get excited about things. If I spot a rare bird, I will excitedly tell someone about it. If I watch a baseball game, I can barely stay in my seat. If I give a talk, I do so with considerable gusto. This tendency of mine toward exuberance did not go unnoticed by the Jesuits with whom I worked for six years. Whenever I got very excited about something, one of them would say to me teasingly, "Melannie, you're gushing again!"

But is "gushing" such a bad thing? Must exuberance always be curbed? I think not. In fact, exuberance is another gift of the Holy Spirit—only we usually call it zeal. The word "zeal" in Greek means "intense heat." In Hebrew, the word denotes the flush that comes to the face of someone experiencing strong emotion. Unfortunately, the word "zeal" has gotten a bad connotation. For some, it connotes only anger. For others, it conjures up images of religious fanatics who scream dire predictions on street corners, shove leaflets into your face at airports, or (worse yet) bomb abortion clinics.

But zeal can be good. Consider this ancient story from the Desert Fathers. It seems Abbot Lot went to see Abbot Joseph and said, "Father, according as I am able, I keep my little rule, and my little fast, my prayer, meditation and contemplative silence. And according as I am able, I strive to cleanse my heart of bad thoughts. Now what more should I do?" The elder rose up in reply and stretched out his hands to heaven, and his fingers became like lamps of fire. He said, "Why not become all flame?"

Zeal is about "becoming all flame." It is about being on fire with God's love. If we page through Scripture, we find numerous individuals who were zealous and exuberant, who became all flame.

Take David. When David became king of Israel, he comported himself in a kingly, dignified manner—most of the time. But when the Ark of the Covenant was brought to Jerusalem, David was so happy he couldn't control his exuberance (2 Samuel 6). Hearing the horns, harps, and cymbals, he ran out of the palace, whipped off his crown, threw off his kingly robes, and danced with abandon in the streets with the people. We can picture him jumping up and down, swaying back and forth, laughing and singing—in little more than his underwear. As David danced with joy in the street, his wife Michal watched in disgust from a window. In fact, she became furious with David—so much so that she "despised him in her heart."

Later that day, when David returned to the palace, he was confronted by his raging wife who cried out, "How could you do such a thing?! Dancing like that—in only your shorts! You made a fool of yourself before all the people, you idiot!" (That's a very free translation.) But David replied, "What do you mean, woman? I was dancing before the ark of the Lord! And I will continue to make merry before the Lord any time I want to! So there!" (Another free translation.) David refused to let anyone curb his exuberance for the Lord.

Another person who was exuberant was Mary. When she visited her cousin Elizabeth, she broke out into song, proclaiming all the marvelous things God had done for her and her people. Mary must have passed on some of that exuberance to her son. For the fact is, the effectiveness of Jesus' preaching was largely due to the exuberance with which he spoke, a passion that amazed even his enemies. After Jesus' ascension, the apostles got their own taste of the exuberance that comes from the Spirit. At Pentecost, they became so inflamed with zeal, that the crowd, upon hearing them speak, thought they were drunk!

Comportment has its place, yes. But, when it comes to expressing our love for God and passing on our faith, zeal and exuberance have their place, too. There are times we must resist the pressure to behave, to keep our voices down, to sit quietly in our place. Instead, we must let ourselves be carried away by the joy of knowing that the One who is mighty has done marvelous things for us! Let's dance!

Have I ever met anyone who was "all flame"? How exuberant am I at expressing and passing on my faith?

✠ Exuberant Spirit, grace me with the gift of zeal today!

INDEX

Index of Topics

(Topics in **bold print** are the titles of the chapters. These are arranged alphabetically in the book. Other topics listed below are cross-references to these chapters.)

BIBLIOGRAPHY

Bibliography

Bausch, William J. *A World of Stories for Preachers and Teachers.* Mystic,CT: Twenty-Third Publications, 1998.

Bender, Sue. *Everyday Sacred.* San Francisco: HarperSanFrancisco, 1995.

Borg, Marcus. *Meeting Jesus Again for the First Time.* New York: HarperCollins, 1994.

Buechner, Frederick. *Wishful Thinking: A Theological ABC.* New York: Harper and Row, 1973.

Burghardt, Walter. *Seasons that Laugh or Weep: Musings on the Human Journey.* New York: Paulist Press, 1983.

Ciardi, John. *The Collected Poems.* Fayetteville, AK: The University of Arkansas Press, 1997.

De Mello, Anthony, SJ. *Taking Flight: A Book of Story Meditations.* New York: Doubleday, 1988.

Dillard, Annie. *The Writing Life.* New York: Harper & Row, 1989.

Heschel, Abraham. *I Asked for Wonder: A Spiritual Anthology.* ed. Samuel H. Dresner. New York: Crossroad, 1983.

Dumm, Demetrius, OSB. *Cherish Christ Above All.* New York: Paulist Press, 1996.

Farrell, Edward. *Surprised by the Spirit.* Denville, NJ: Dimension Books, 1973.

Gendler, J. Ruth. *The Book of Qualities.* Berkeley, CA: Turquoise Mountain Publications, 1984.

Green, Thomas, SJ. *Weeds Among the Wheat.* Notre Dame, IN: Ave Maria Press, 1984.

Hample, Stuart and Eric Marshall. *Children's Letters to God.* New York: Workman Publishing, 1991.

Keating, Thomas. *Intimacy with God.* New York: Crossroad, 1994.

Krisher, James A. *Spiritual Surrender: Yielding Yourself to a Loving God.* Mystic, CT: Twenty-Third Publications, 1997.

Lamott, Anne. *Bird by Bird.* New York: Doubleday, 1994.

_____. *Operating Instructions: A Journal of My Son's First Year.* New York: Pantheon, 1993.

Leimbach, Patricia. *The Thread of Blue Denim.* Englewood Cliffs, NJ: Prentice-Hall, 1974.

Léon-Dufour, Xavier. *Dictionary of the New Testament.* San Francisco: Harper & Row, 1980.

_____. *Dictionary of Biblical Theology.* New York: Seabury Press, 1973.

Lewis, C.S. *A Grief Observed.* New York: Seabury Press, 1976.

Marty, Martin and Micah Marty. *When True Simplicity Is Gained.* Grand Rapids, MI: William B. Eerdmans Publishing Company, 1998.

McBrien, Richard, gen. ed. *Encyclopedia of Catholicism.* San Francisco: HarperCollins, 1995.

McKenzie, John, SJ. *Dictionary of the Bible.* Milwaukee: Bruce Publishing Co., 1965.

Moore, Thomas. *Care of the Soul.* New York: HarperPerennial, 1994.

Morneau, Robert. *Fathoming Bethlehem.* New York: Crossroad, 1997.

Norris, Kathleen. *Amazing Grace: A Vocabulary of Faith.* New York: Riverhead Books, 1998.

Padovano, Anthony. *Who Is Christ?* Notre Dame, IN: Ave Maria Press, 1967.

Paton, Alan. *For You Departed.* New York: Charles Scribner's Sons, 1969.

Pieper, Josef. *Leisure: The Basis of Culture.* New York: Mentor Books,1952.

Senior, Donald, CP. *Jesus: A Gospel Portrait.* Dayton, OH: Pflaum Press, 1975.

Vanderhaar, Gerard. *Beyond Violence.* Mystic, CT: Twenty-Third Publications, 1998.

Wakefield, Gordon, ed. *The Westminster Dictionary of Christian Spirituality.* Philadelphia: Westminster Press, 1983.

Wiederkehr, Macrina, OSB. *Seasons of Your Heart.* Morristown, NJ: Silver Burdett, 1979.

Also by Melannie Svoboda...

Rummaging for God
Seeking the Holy in Every Nook and Cranny

Sister Melannie is a master of metaphor. In this wonderful book she uses the image of rummaging to build a series of meditations on how to find God in everyday events. *Rummaging for God* contains 100 rummagings, that is, short meditations that grew out of the author's own experience. The questions and the short closing prayers at the end of each meditation, as well as the source and topic indexes, help facilitate the reader's own rummaging. Perfect for private prayer and reflection or for group sharing.

ISBN: 0-89622-943-2, 136 pages, $9.95

Everyday Epiphanies
Seeing the Sacred in Every Thing

These 175 short reflections are divided according to the seasons of the year, and each ends with a reflection prayer. Topics range from the mundane to the unusual and unexpected, and each reflection invites readers to discover God in every aspect of life. Scripture passages scattered throughout offer insights into the ways that Jesus used the occurrences of everyday living to reveal both God and grace.

ISBN: 0-89622-730-8, 192 pp, $9.95

Traits of a Healthy Spirituality

Here Sr. Melannie describes twenty indicators of a healthy spirituality, including: self-esteem, friendship, courage, tolerance, joy, and forgiveness. She demonstrates how to use these signs to determine where we stand in terms of our Christian spirituality. Includes meditations, questions for reflection, and closing prayers.

ISBN: 0-89622-698-0, 144 pp, $9.95

Teaching is Like...
Peeling Back Eggshells

Warm and witty, these fifty reflections will sustain enthusiasm, bolster morale, and encourage teaching as a gracefilled privilege.

ISBN: 0-89622-613-1, 120 pp, $7.95

Available at religious bookstores or from:

TWENTY-THIRD PUBLICATIONS

PO BOX 180 • 185 WILLOW STREET MYSTIC, CT 06355 • 1-800-321-0411
FAX: 1-800-572-0788 BAYARD   E-MAIL: ttpubs@aol.com

Call for a free catalog